REMODELI
KITCHENS &
BATHS

REMODELING KITCHENS & BATHS

R. DODGE WOODSON

STERLING PUBLISHING CO., INC.   NEW YORK

This book is dedicated both to my daughter, Afton Amber, and to my wife, Kimberley. My wife has also been my best friend for thirteen years, and Afton is my inspiration. These two *are* my life.

Library of Congress Cataloging-in-Publication Data

Woodson, R. Dodge (Roger Dodge), 1955–
    Remodeling kitchens & baths / by R. Dodge Woodson.
        p.   cm.
    Includes index.
    ISBN 0-8069-8738-3 (pbk.)
    1. Kitchens—Remodeling—Amateurs' manuals.   2. Bathrooms—
Remodeling—Amateurs' manuals.   I. Title   II. Title: Remodeling
kitchens and baths.
TH4816.3.K58W66   1994
643'.3—dc20   93-38648
                                                                    CIP

10 9 8 7 6 5 4 3 2 1

Published by Sterling Publishing Company, Inc.
387 Park Avenue South, New York, N.Y. 10016
© 1994 by R. Dodge Woodson
Distributed in Canada by Sterling Publishing
% Canadian Manda Group, P.O. Box 920, Station U
Toronto, Ontario, Canada M8Z 5P9
Distributed in Great Britain and Europe by Cassell PLC
Villiers House, 41/47 Strand, London WC2N 5JE, England
Distributed in Australia by Capricorn Link (Australia) Pty Ltd.
P.O. Box 6651, Baulkham Hills, Business Centre, NSW 2153, Australia
Manufactured in the United States of America
All rights reserved

Sterling ISBN 0-8069-8738-3

Contents

CONTENTS

CONTENTS

Preface

Kitchen and bathroom remodeling both offer some of the best opportunities for return on home-improvement investment. These two types of remodeling are proven winners, and they sometimes produce more value than their cost.

This book is written for the do-it-yourselfer. If you want to remodel your kitchen or bathroom, this book will provide almost all of the technical help you'll need. You'll find in these pages the facts and the experience that I've gained during my twenty-year career in the construction and remodeling businesses.

In addition to the text, you'll find hundreds of illustrations between these pages to make your job easier. Whether you're embarking on your first remodeling project or you're a seasoned veteran of the remodeling industry, you'll find that this volume will be invaluable during your kitchen or bathroom remodeling, because you'll be shown how to remodel from start to finish. Several chapters deal with the planning stages, the demolition work, and the reconstruction.

Successful remodeling is often a product of experience and knowledge. I've been in the building trades for twenty years, and I've done many, many remodeling jobs. During those twenty years I've made many mistakes, and that's to your advantage. Rather than learning from *your* mistakes, you can learn from *mine* and save yourself pain, frustration, and money.

After you've remodeled, all that's left is to decorate. Decorating is fun, and it's important. The right decor will enhance your attractive new space.

By the time you get to the decorating stage, this book should be well used. Rather than explaining decorating ideas to you in words, I'll accomplish this task with photos. Of the 51 color photos interspersed throughout this book, most are meant solely to provide you with ideas that may transform your decorating project from good to great!

I'm a licensed contractor, a licensed master plumber, and a licensed real-estate broker. I've seen remodeling from all angles, and I'll share my knowledge with you in the following chapters.

1
Planning

Proper planning is the key to success in any remodeling venture. If you make an error when planning, the results could be both dissatisfying and costly.

Planning is critical to a successful remodeling job for several reasons. It allows you to establish a budget, a timetable, and a goal for the desired results. For example, if you'll be working on a limited budget it will be necessary to separate your needs from your desires.

Establishing an accurate timetable can be crucial. If you have only one bathroom in your home, knowing how long you won't be able to use it will let you make alternative arrangements. Since few homes have more than one kitchen, a major kitchen remodeling can mean many trips to restaurants. The timetable for remodeling your kitchen not only affects how much you'll be inconvenienced, it also affects the overall cost of the job; those trips to restaurants can be expensive.

Before you begin to tear out kitchen cabinets or bathtubs, have a plan for their replacements. Don't begin a major remodeling job without a plan for the end result. Imagine ripping out your kitchen cabinets only to find that the replacement cabinets you thought would be immediately available would actually take six weeks to get? Could you live without a kitchen for six weeks?

Planning a major remodeling job isn't something you do in one afternoon; proper planning takes time and effort. There will be phone calls to make, specifications to draft, and much more. This chapter will show you, step by step, what to do and how to do it. To begin planning your remodeling job, study the format for planning a sample job, found in this chapter.

Needs & Desires

Remodeling jobs evolve either from needs or from desires; you should know the difference between needs and desires before you make financial commitments.

The kitchen is normally considered the most important room in a home to remodel, and bathrooms are considered the second-best room to remodel. If you review statistics on which types of remodeling jobs are most likely to pay for themselves when a home is sold, you'll see that kitchens and bathrooms usually rank first and second. While it's true that bathrooms and kitchens are great places to invest your home-improvement money, invest wisely. You could lose money by overinvesting, or by installing unconventional products or materials.

Kitchens and bathrooms are both expected to have certain components. Bathrooms are expected to have toilets, lavatories, and bathing units. Kitchens should be equipped with cabinets, counters, sinks, and appliances. In addition to the essentials, there are many add-on products available, especially for kitchens, that really aren't mandatory. Separate your *needs* from your *desires*. See Illustrations 1-1 through 1-11 for examples of such add-ons.

Assume that you want to update a standard bathroom. The bathroom has a wall-

Illus. 1-1. Pull-out base storage unit for bathroom vanities. Photo courtesy of Decora'

Illus. 1-2. Under-cabinet lighting. Photo courtesy of Lis King Public Relations

Illus. 1-3. An overhead microwave oven above and an indoor grill below. Photo courtesy of Jenn-Air Company

Illus. 1-4. An indoor grill and a cooktop. Photo courtesy of Jenn-Air Company

Illus. 1-5. A tip-out bathroom vanity hamper.
Photo courtesy of Decora'

Illus. 1-6. A utility slide-out storage cabinet.
Photo courtesy of Decora′

Illus. 1-7. Base-cabinet bottle storage. Photo courtesy of Decora'

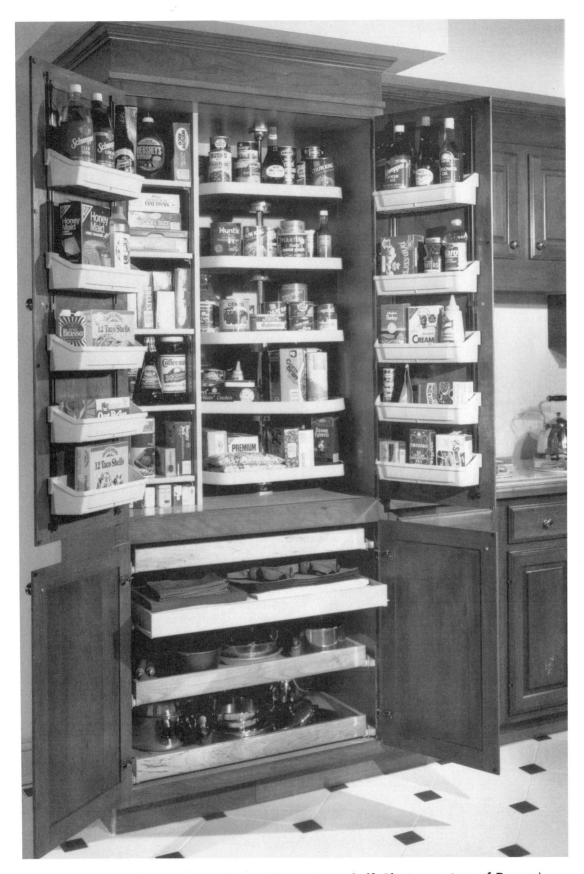

Illus. 1-8. A utility storage cabinet with a rotary shelf. Photo courtesy of Decora′

Illus. 1-9. A mesh organizer rack. Photo courtesy of Clairson International

Illus. 1-10. Slide-out baskets. Photo courtesy of Clairson International

Illus. 1-11. A pull-out cabinet for trash bins and recycling receptacles. Photo courtesy of Lis King Public Relations

hung lavatory, a two-piece toilet, and a bathtub without a shower. The existing floor is in good condition, but the old vinyl flooring is worn and dull. The walls and ceiling are painted drywall, and there is an old, metal medicine cabinet, with a mirror, over the lavatory. The room is functional, but aesthetically unpleasing. What will you do to give this room a face-lift?

If you want to make a safe investment, you won't get fancy options; you'll make improvements, but they'll be simple and relatively inexpensive. For example, you'll replace the toilet with a new two-piece toilet. The wall-hung lavatory will be replaced with a modest vanity with a marble-look top. New faucets will be installed for the lavatory and bathing unit, and the old tub will be replaced with a sectional tub/shower unit. You'll repaint the walls and ceiling, and replace the old vinyl with new. The metal medicine cabinet will be replaced with an attractive wood-frame cabinet and mirror

(Illus. 1-12). The fluorescent light that was once over the old medicine cabinet will be replaced with a three-light oak light strip (Illus. 1-13).

The bathroom would then be modernized and functional, but neither luxurious nor expensive. This type of remodeling would meet all common needs, and it would be likely to return all of its cost when you sell your house.

But, suppose you want to replace the old bathtub with a whirlpool tub (Illustrations 1-14, 1-15); how would that affect your job? Unless you have health problems, the whirlpool must be considered a desire, not a need. The extra expense of the whirlpool might be recoverable when you sell your house, but then again, it might not. Installing such a tub would extend your financial risk.

Perhaps you've always wanted a one-piece toilet and a pedestal lavatory (see the color photo on page 65). These two items

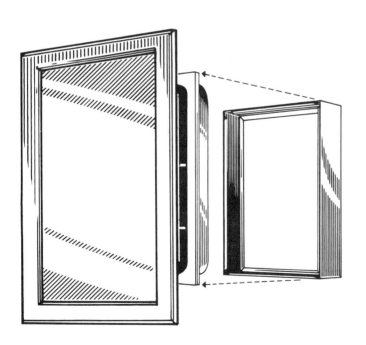

Illus. 1-12. Recessed medicine cabinet with a wood frame and a mirror. Drawing printed with permission of NuTone, Inc., Cincinnati, Ohio 45227

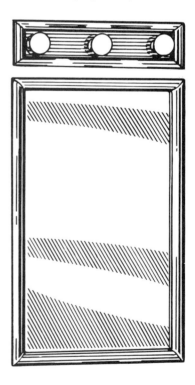

Illus. 1-13. Three-light strip light. Drawing printed with permission of NuTone, Inc., Cincinnati, Ohio 45227

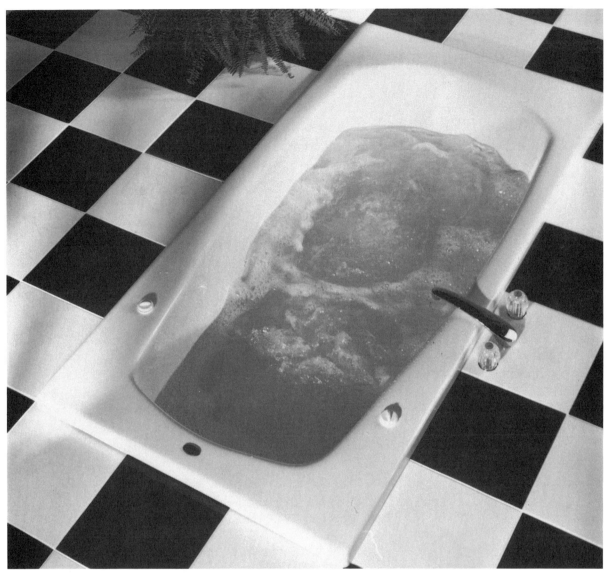

Illus. 1-14. Whirlpool tub. Photo courtesy of Lis King Public Relations

are desires, not needs. The bathroom would function just as well with a simple lavatory and a simple toilet as it would with fancy fixtures. The extra money you spend on a pedestal lavatory and one-piece toilet may not really add to the value of your bathroom. The added expense is fine, but realize that the added money may not be recovered, and that you're buying items you *want*, not items you *need*.

This type of "needs vs. desires" evaluation will enable you to realize your goals without exceeding your budget. Get excited about getting a new kitchen or bathroom, but temper that excitement with logic and sound judgment. Don't allow your dreams to exceed your financial capabilities.

A Viable Budget

Arriving at a viable budget for remodeling isn't always easy. Each time you visit a store, or thumb through a remodeling magazine, your want list can grow. Unless money is no

Illus. 1-15. A whirlpool tub surrounded by glass blocks. Photo courtesy of Pittsburgh Corning Corp.

object, self-discipline must prevail over sudden emotion. A viable budget will take time and effort to achieve, but it will also protect you from financial disaster.

How Can a Budget Protect You?

A budget, broken down by categories, will define the limits for each type of expense involved with your job. For example, if you've budgeted a certain amount for a stainless-steel kitchen sink, you shouldn't buy a much more expensive cast-iron sink with a high-fashion color. Set up your budget in phases to keep your spending on track.

A good budget will start at the beginning and include every phase of work to be done. It will be broken down into several categories, and it will be laid out to show projected costs and actual costs.

The more detailed the budget breakdowns are, the better. For example, you could have a broad category, like plumbing, or you could break down that broad category into smaller sections, such as subcategories for labor, fixtures, and rough materials. This breakdown would be helpful if you do your own plumbing, but if you hire a contractor the budget breakdown might be different.

When you hire a contractor, you'll work with prices he quoted you for the services and materials he provides. In this case, the breakdown between labor and rough materials isn't very important. However, it would be wise to include a budget amount for each plumbing fixture. Looking at lump-sum figures isn't always as graphic as seeing the costs broken down. If you see quotes from three plumbers for a certain lump-sum amount, you might mumble about the high cost, but you won't know if the price could be changed. When you see that you are paying so much for a toilet, so much for a bathtub, and so much for a vanity and top, you can evaluate options and alternatives. Seeing individual prices will allow you to manipulate your plans to maintain your budget.

If you don't establish a viable budget, costs could get out of hand. Before you start writing checks and charging materials, you should know (within a reasonable range) what your total expenditures will be.

Financing

Bathroom and kitchen remodeling can be very expensive, and for most people this means borrowing money. While some detest the idea of financing *anything*, some types of home-improvement financing may be to your advantage.

Equity Loans

Getting an equity loan on your home could result in some tax advantages. It's possible that the interest paid on this type of loan is tax-deductible. If you can find financing that offers tax advantages and then you invest your cash wisely in other areas, you may actually come out ahead of the game.

"In-Home" Financing

Many contractors have relationships with lenders. The rates and terms of this type of loan usually aren't as good as those you could obtain from your own bank, but there are times when an "in-home" loan may be justified. If you decide to accept in-home financing, make sure you understand all of the terms and conditions. Have a lawyer review the paperwork and have him give you an opinion of the loan before you sign.

Plans & Specifications

While simple remodeling won't require the use of complex blueprints, you must have a set of plans (even if they're only simple line drawings) and specifications for the work you want done, especially if you'll be using contractors.

It's impossible to obtain accurate bids from contractors unless you provide them with plans and specifications. If you don't provide them with detailed plans and specifications, the contractors may all bid on the job based on their individual different interpretations. The result may be bids that can't be fairly compared.

Some people just aren't able to draw working plans, but all homeowners can create detailed *specifications* for their jobs. You can have professionals draw your plans for you, but you must create your own specifications since nobody else knows what things you want. This part of your planning is essential, and it should be done before you seek bids for labor and materials.

Planning for Inconvenience

Planning for inconvenience is part of any remodeling job, but it's especially applicable to kitchens and bathrooms. If you converted your basement to finished living space, you'd have to put up with noise, dust, and the traffic of contractors, but the level of inconvenience involved with kitchen and bath remodeling exceeds that of most other forms of remodeling.

When your kitchen is torn apart and reduced to a subfloor and bare walls, it can make life a little awkward. If the only toilet in your house has been removed to allow the installation of new floor coverings, you may wish you knew your neighbors better.

To avoid going hungry or using your neighbor's bathroom, plan for inconveniences. If your plans call for a total bathroom renovation, it's logical to assume that you may be without a bathtub for a few days. Your toilet could be out of service for several hours at a time, and your lavatory may not be back in working order for days.

In the case of major kitchen renovations, cooking may be out of the question for several days, or even weeks. When your old kitchen cabinets are removed, where will you put all the items that had been stored in them? Having contractors stand around, mumbling and tapping their feet, while you box up food, utensils, and small appliances can be stressful. Proper planning will allow you to avoid this stressful (and somewhat embarrassing) situation.

Sit down and draw a mental picture of how the job will progress. If you don't know enough about what will be done to create a plausible picture, ask your contractors to explain the sequence of events. If necessary, outline the work on a piece of paper to help you to anticipate and avoid complications. For example, assume the electrical wiring in your kitchen will be updated. What will happen to the food in your refrigerator and freezer? Can you use an extension cord to keep the appliances running, or will you have to make other arrangements for your perishable foods?

There's much more to major remodeling jobs than what you first might think. Look ahead, plan carefully, and be prepared for unexpected changes to avoid many problems and to prepare for some unavoidable trouble.

A Realistic Timetable

Remodeling jobs rarely go as planned, and staying on schedule can be very difficult. If one aspect of the job is delayed, the whole job can be affected. For example, if the kitchen countertop isn't delivered on time, the plumber won't be able to install the kitchen sink, the garbage disposer, or the dishwasher. The delay in installing the disposer and dishwasher will throw off the electrician's schedule, and the chain of events can go on and on. If the cabinet delivery is delayed, the whole job can grind to a halt.

There are many circumstances that no individual can control fully, so organizing a workable completion schedule won't be easy. The best you can do is to create a schedule and to strive to maintain it. This may mean hounding contractors or suppliers to do what they've promised. Jobs don't run themselves; if they did, you wouldn't need general contractors.

A production schedule can be achieved, if the deadlines are realistic. Allow adequate time for each phase of work, and the chances are good that you can meet your self-imposed deadlines. There will be times when you can't control delays. Some jobs are plagued with bad luck: The wrong cabinets will be shipped, the bathtub will be damaged, the painter won't show up for days, and so on. Is this just bad luck or is it bad planning? Usually it's a deficiency in organizational skills and follow-up effort, but there are times when even your best efforts can't solve the problems.

While you can't control all aspects of your job, there is much you can do to keep it on schedule. For example, if you inspect all materials as soon as they're delivered, you'll avoid some loss of time. If you have your tub delivered ahead of time, for example, and you spot damage immediately, you can avoid lost time.

How to Set Realistic Time Goals

If you hire contractors to do your job, ask them how long their portions of the job will take. Consult cost-estimating manuals that give estimates for the time needed to complete various phases of work. Compare the data in the estimating manual with the answers given by your contractors. If the two estimates are similar, you should be right on track. When the time estimates differ substantially, investigate further. For example, if you examine three bids from three electricians, and one says that the job will take two days, ask the other electricians how long they believe the work will take. Once you have their three time projections, you can answer your own question about the time required to complete that phase of the job.

A form can be used to list each phase of work to be done and the estimated time allowed for the work. If you do the work yourself, setting a completion date will be a little more difficult. However, you can still use cost-estimating manuals to help determine your time needs. Many of these guides list the number of hours a job should take to complete when professionals do the work. Some of the guides give advice on how to adjust the time estimates to allow for lack of professional experience.

Remodeling jobs almost always take longer to complete than anyone (except seasoned remodelers) expects. Once you've outlined a production schedule, build in some extra time for unexpected delays. For example, when you remove the floor covering in your bathroom, you may find that the subfloor and floor joists have been damaged by a water leak at the base of the toilet. This type of unexpected work will increase the cost of your job and the time it takes to complete the job. Build in a buffer for unexpected problems and mistakes in time estimates, and you'll be likely to finish on or ahead of schedule.

Contractors

Contractors may also play a significant role in the success of your remodeling project. Choosing the right contractors isn't always easy, but it's absolutely necessary. The wrong choice of contractors can turn your remodeling dream into a nightmare.

Any contractor you hire should be properly licensed and insured; you may even find it beneficial to work with bonded contractors. Don't take chances with part-timers who are neither licensed nor insured; the risks far outweigh the advantages. What would happen if you hired an uninsured plumber and the plumber's torch burned your house down? Suppose an uninsured electrician made a mistake that resulted in a fatal shock, or a fire. These are just two possibilities for potential disasters if you hire uninsured contractors.

If the workers aren't licensed, the work may not be done in accordance with local building-code requirements. Since permits and inspections are required for many aspects of kitchen and bath remodeling, work with contractors who'll abide by the codes. Failure to comply with the codes could result in mandatory removal of the illegally installed work, cash fines, and other penalties. This could add up to financial losses far in excess of the money you saved by using unlicensed workers.

If you hire contractors, choose them carefully. Check their references, inquire with local agencies that report complaints against contractors, and don't give the contractors large deposits for the work to be done. If you give them money before they've earned it, you may never see it again.

Final Results

Knowing what you want as the end result of your remodeling is also important. Are you doing the job to build equity in your home, or just to satisfy your personal preferences? It's possible to do both at the same time, but the two don't necessarily go together. If you want to build equity in your home by remodeling a kitchen or bathroom, be selective in the work you do.

Spending too much on improvements can negate any equity you hope to build. But, if you're making the changes to suit your personal desires, and you're not worried about recovering your investment, as long as you can afford it, you can do it.

Decide what you hope to gain from your remodeling. Do you want more light in your kitchen? Must you have a whirlpool tub to make your life complete? Will doing the work yourself and building several thousand dollars of equity in your home make you happy? Allow adequate time to find the real reasons for your urge to remodel. If you dedicate enough time to planning your project, you're much more likely to get pleasing results.

2
Understanding Blueprints & Design Plans

If you plan an extensive remodeling job, you'll benefit from a good understanding of blueprints and design plans. While complex drawings are rarely used in minor remodeling jobs, they are common in larger jobs. If you expand your kitchen and relocate your fixtures, appliances, and cabinets, you should have a detailed set of plans. Solid working plans are essential if you want contractors to do the job the way you want.

Many homeowners choose to save some money by not having professional blueprints prepared for their remodeling jobs. Sometimes these homeowners are able to communicate what they want to contractors and are able to get what they want. But many times communication between the parties isn't very good, and the job doesn't turn out as the homeowner had hoped.

If you do a major remodeling job, plans and specifications should be considered a compulsory expense. The money or time you spend preparing precise plans and specifications can save you time, money, and aggravation.

It's easy for two people to see the same thing differently. For example, you tell your plumber that you want an almond-colored, two-piece toilet. You leave for work, and nine or ten hours later, when you get home, the plumber has installed an almond-colored, two-piece toilet. You take one look at it and hate it. What will you do? The plumber provided what you asked for, it just isn't what you thought it would be.

There are many styles of toilets, and some prefer one style over another. While the toilet the plumber installed is a name-brand and is commonly used, it doesn't look like what you thought it would. If you'd given the plumber a make and model number, you'd have gotten the toilet you wanted. Now you've got a toilet you don't want, but you can't expect the plumber to replace it for free; after all, it does meet the description you gave him. Because of situations like these, detailed specifications are needed on *all* jobs.

How Can Blueprints Help?

Blueprints will act as a "road map" for all work being done. Let's say you're remodeling your kitchen and having an island cabinet installed; the island will hold a vented indoor grill (Illus. 2-1).

Assume that you'll be doing this job without the aid of blueprints. Before you leave for work, you point with your finger to a place where you want the carpenters to install the island. You speak with the carpenters, electricians, and appliance installers, and you feel that you have the installation of the island and grill well defined, and then you leave for work.

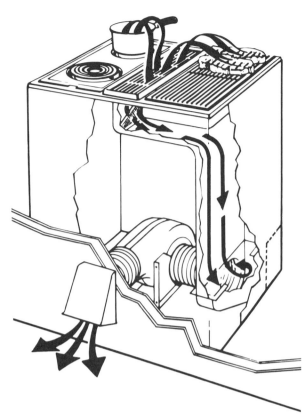

Illus. 2-1. Vented indoor grill. Drawing courtesy of Jenn-Air Company

Nine or ten hours later, when you return home, the island and grill are installed, but what have your workers done? The doors on the island cabinet are on the wrong side, and the grill is in the top *backwards*. The island is where you told the workers to put it, it's just not facing the direction you thought it would be. You knew which way you wanted everything installed, but you failed to tell the contractors.

Since the unit is now installed permanently, it will be expensive to alter. The alteration would involve duct work, electrical work, and carpentry work. You can't expect the contractors to perform the work free of charge, but to get the island the way you want it, the work must be done. You've just exceeded your budget because of poor communication. A detailed set of blueprints would have prevented this problem.

When Are Blueprints Needed?

Blueprints, or at least line drawings, are beneficial to all jobs, but they're almost a necessity for large jobs.

Minor Bath Remodeling

Minor bath remodeling doesn't require extensive blueprints. The job can be done without any drawings, but it may help to have a simple line drawing that depicts the finished project.

Assume that you won't be changing the location of any primary plumbing, but that you will be replacing all of your plumbing fixtures. If new fixtures will be installed in the exact locations of the existing fixtures, it shouldn't be necessary to have blueprints to indicate fixture placement. Putting a new bathtub in the old opening and setting a new toilet on an existing flange doesn't require much instruction.

If all of the work in this job will be as obvious, plans won't be needed, but good specifications will. There are many times when detailed drawings can be avoided, but never hire contractors to do a job without explicit specifications.

Kitchen Expansion

Kitchen expansion is one form of remodeling that should be done with the help of good blueprints or line drawings (Illustrations 2-2, 2-3, 2-4, 2-5). This type of work involves many changes and many opportunities for confusion. If you build an addition onto your home to expand the kitchen, blueprints will be very important.

When you change fixture locations, cabinet locations, wall locations, and so forth, detailed plans should be used. Unless the job is so obvious that no one could make a mistake, plans should be used.

Many building-code enforcement offices will not issue permits for work to be done

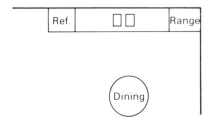

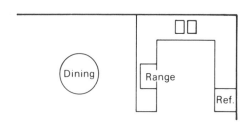

Illus. 2-2. A sidewall-type kitchen. Line drawing courtesy of USDA Forest Service

Illus. 2-3. A galley-type kitchen. Line drawing courtesy of USDA Forest Service

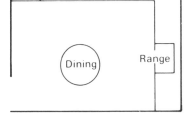

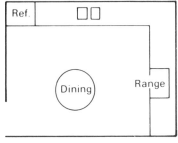

Illus. 2-4. An "L"-type kitchen. Line drawing courtesy of USDA Forest Service

Illus. 2-5. A "U"-type kitchen. Line drawing courtesy of USDA Forest Service

until they're provided with plans and specifications. So even if you don't want a set of plans, you may have to have them drawn in order to obtain necessary permits.

Reading Blueprints

Reading blueprints isn't difficult if you take your time and you understand the symbols used on the drawings. In the case of most kitchen and bath remodeling jobs, the blueprints won't be very complicated. However, you'll still need to understand how plans are drawn to scale and what the various symbols mean.

If you work from a set of professionally drawn blueprints, everything you need to know to read them is likely to be included on the plans. There should be notes that

indicate what scale is being used on the plans, and there should be a section that shows what all the symbols mean.

Learning what the symbols and different types of lines represent isn't difficult. Working with scale drawings is easiest when you have a scale ruler, but any ruler will do. Most blueprints are drawn with a scale where a ¼″ on the blueprint is equal to one foot in real life. In other words, a countertop that measures 2″ on this type of blueprint would actually be 8′ long.

Not all blueprints are drawn to the same scale. In fact, it's possible for the scale to change from one page of the prints to the next. The scale often changes for cross-section details and elevations. Before relying on scale measurements, check each section of the plans for the scale being used.

If you do the work yourself, professionally drawn blueprints will be your guide. By checking the prints, you can see what size lumber is required, how thick the countertop should be, how far below the ceiling the cabinets should hang, and where the fixtures should be placed. A good set of blueprints will leave nothing to the imagination.

Specifications

If you work as a do-it-yourselfer, professionally prepared specifications can be helpful. While you may know that an underlayment is needed for your new tile floor, you may not know what size or type of underlayment to use. Professional specifications will tell you which materials to use.

If you think you don't need clear specifications when you do the work yourself, you're probably wrong. Even professionals rely on specifications drafted by architects and engineers. You might know how to install a floor joist, but it's quite another thing to know what size joist to install. Every job benefits from clear specifications, regardless of who's doing the work.

When you hire others to remodel for you, having detailed specifications is the only way to ensure that you'll get the job done the way you want it done. If you provide a carpenter with a detailed set of plans and specifications and the job doesn't turn out right, you can insist that changes be made, at no cost to you, to bring the job into compliance with the plans and specifications. You should have each contractor sign a copy of the plans and specifications to prove that he or she was given a set; this procedure can be of great benefit if you're one of the unfortunate few who goes to court to confront a cantankerous contractor.

Patience

The key to understanding blueprints and design plans is patience. Take your time when looking at the plans, and familiarize yourself with the symbols and scales. Practice scaling distances on lines where the distances are given. If you see a wall with a noted length of 8', scale it and see if you come up with the right measurement. Always confirm the scale on the section of drawing that you're working with. Look at the legend of symbols and search the plans until you can find and identify each one. Practice makes perfect when reading blueprints.

3
Sketching Your Intentions

When you plan to remodel, sketch your intentions. Having a sketch of what you want will make planning much easier. You don't have to be an architect to draw your own preliminary plans.

Line drawings are often very effective tools for interior remodeling jobs. If you won't be making structural changes in your home, a simple line drawing may be all you need to get the job done. Even if you have no artistic ability, you can probably do a fair job of sketching a rough plan with the help of a ruler and some graph paper.

If your job is complex enough to warrant cross-sections and elevations that you're unable to draw, there are many options for you to consider. You could use an architect, but plans drawn by architects are usually very expensive.

Imagine that you're going to remodel a kitchen, but you're not sure what you want the new kitchen to look like (Illustrations 3-1 through 3-5). Where should you start your planning? It would be nice to look through a book of floor plans, but few such books contain only kitchen plans.

House-plan books also contain kitchen and bathroom plans. The kitchen and bathroom plans are not drawn individually; they're part of the overall house plan. During the planning stage of a remodeling job, you're likely to be looking for ideas, and these plan books can provide you with many ideas. Because there are so many choices, your chief problem will be to decide on *which* ideas to incorporate into your personal plans.

A single book of house plans may contain more than one hundred different bathroom and kitchen layouts. When you consider how many different books of plans are available, you might find thousands of designs to work with. Many of the designs will be similar, but each will have its own special features. Borrow from several plans to come up with an ideal plan for your kitchen or bathroom.

When you look at the floor plans for the various kitchens and bathrooms, notice how simple they are. Most of them will consist only of simple lines (some may be drawn in a dimensional perspective). Couldn't you draw similar plans with the help of a few drafting tools and some graph paper?

Sketch Your Own Plans

Gather a few basic drafting instruments, and you can make your drawings look like those found in plan books. There are templates available that allow you to draw sinks, toilets, and doors with ease. An architectural scale ruler is inexpensive, and it makes scaling a drawing very easy. If you don't want to buy a scale ruler, you can use any ruler to create your own scale drawing. The grids on graph paper make scaling a rough drawing possible for anyone. You *can* draw your own preliminary plans.

Templates

Inexpensive templates are available for each symbol you see on a floor plan. Win-

Illus. 3-1. U-shaped kitchen. Drawing courtesy of Merillat Industries

dows, doors, sinks, lavatories, toilets, bathtubs, and other items can be drawn with these plastic guides. Hold the template on the paper and trace a pencil around it.

Scale Rulers

Scale rulers are inexpensive, and they make drawing and working with scaled drawings much easier than using a standard ruler. Get an architectural scale ruler; it will be of the most use to you for construction blueprints.

Scale rulers are equipped to handle several different scales. It won't matter whether you work with a ¼″ scale or a ½″ scale, your scale ruler will convert the scale to real measurements. Lay the ruler on a line and measure it. If you're working with a ¼″ scale, a 3″ line will read as 12′ on the scale ruler.

Ordinary rulers can be used to work with scale drawings, but you'll have to do the

Illus. 3-2. Island kitchen. Drawing courtesy of Merillat Industries

math conversions on your own. Such conversions consume time, and they make mistakes likely.

Graph paper

Graph paper is the best type of paper to use for your preliminary drawing. The paper will have grids; assign each of these grids a value. For example, you might say the distance between horizontal lines equals one foot, or you could say it equals one inch.

Once you have graph paper, a ruler, and a pencil, draw a rough plan of what you want to do. Having a template for your symbols will make the drawing look more professional, but you can do without the template. Equipped with these tools, it takes almost no artistic ability to draw a simple floor plan.

Professional Help

Getting professional help to draw working plans isn't difficult, but it can be expensive. Architects are very well qualified for drawing your plans, but their fees are generally too expensive for simple home remodeling.

Illus. 3-3. L-shaped kitchen. Drawing courtesy of Merillat Industries

Drafting Companies

Many drafting firms draw blueprints and floor plans. Again, if you only need a floor plan, you can do it yourself, but if you are doing extensive remodeling or structural work, you'd be better off with professionally drawn plans. Most drafting companies will draw working plans from your rough drawing for very reasonable prices.

Free Drafting Services

Some building-supply stores will provide free drafting services for their customers. If you're willing to buy your materials from the supplier, there's a good chance that you can get your plans drawn free. However, the free plans may not be the bargain they appear to be. Before you commit to a deal like this, check the supplier's prices and the quality of its materials. It's possible that the price you'll pay for materials is far too much. If this is the case, you may be better off paying someone else to draw your plans, and then you can buy your materials wherever you wish.

College Students

Students who take drafting classes may be able to give you good working plans for a low price.

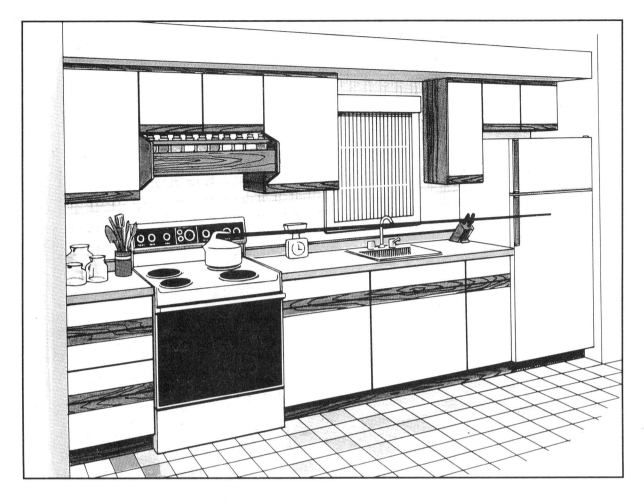

Illus. 3-4. Single-wall kitchen. Drawing courtesy of Merillat Industries

How Accurate Must Preliminary Sketches Be?

There's no rule that says preliminary sketches must be to scale, but if they aren't, it will be easy to lose perspective on the job. It isn't important for the symbols to be exact drafting symbols, but you should strive to maintain a consistent scale.

If you don't draw the floor plan to scale, objects may appear much larger or smaller than they'll actually be. Many homeowners draw a bathroom plan that looks spacious, but without drawing the sketch to scale, this spaciousness may be illusory. If you draw a bathtub freehand, it's easy to draw it to fit any space you want, but in reality, you'll need a space that's five feet wide to install the tub. Many homeowners fail to realize how large vanities, bathtubs, or linen closets (and similar objects) really are. This failure will distort the options available in a given space. To avoid disappointment when construction starts, draw your sketches to scale.

Judging Size

Judging the size of some items can be difficult. Do you know that a typical base cabinet for a kitchen sink is normally 5′ wide? What are standard widths for wall cabinets that aren't custom-made? The most common widths for stock wall cabinets are 12″, 15″, 18″, 24″, 30″, and 36″. How deep are most of these cabinets? The depth of most wall cabinets is 30″. If you'll be remodeling

Illus. 3-5. Galley kitchen. Drawing courtesy of Merillat Industries

a powder room and you need a small vanity, what might be the smallest stock size available? A 16″ × 18″ vanity should be easy to find. Knowing these sizes will be important when you design your new kitchen or bathroom.

How will you know which sizes to use for various items? You could look in catalogs for sizes, or you could go to building-supply centers and measure various items.

Building-Code Requirements

Code requirements are another factor you must consider when drawing your working plans. If you only draw a rough sketch, and you'll have a professional prepare your working plans, you can get by without knowing building-code requirements. The professional designer or draftsman will adjust your drawing to comply with building-code requirements.

Why will building-code requirements af-

fect your drawing? They may influence the layout of your fixtures, outlets, and so on. For example, a toilet requires a clear space 30″ wide for installation. The distance from the front of a toilet to another fixture is normally required to be at least 18″. If you weren't aware of these requirements, you might lay out your bathroom in a way that would violate code requirements, and then you'd have to redesign it.

If you draw your own working plans and submit them for approval to the local building-code enforcement office, the code officer will notify you if the drawing is in violation of the code. Door widths, ceiling heights, electrical outlets, and plumbing fixtures are where most of the spacing requirements will be scrutinized.

Once you've completed your preliminary plans, there will probably be many changes made to them. You should make these changes before work begins, but that isn't always possible.

4
Solidifying Your Plans

Remodeling is known for its unexpected changes in plans, but you should do your best to avoid "in-progress" changes. Even after doing your best, you'll probably experience some problems. Professional remodelers have problems with most jobs, so it's unlikely you won't.

There are many ways to reduce the risks of on-the-job problems. If you'll be using contractors on your job, meet with each of them prior to starting work. One common problem on many jobs is conflict among the different trades. It isn't unusual for plumbers and heating mechanics to get in each other's way. Electricians sometimes block the paths of other trades, and painters and drywall finishers often argue about who is at fault for less-than-perfect wall finishes. Of course, if you do all of the work yourself, there won't be anyone else to worry about.

Most homeowners don't have all of the skills necessary to do a full-scale remodeling job; some professional help is needed. However, any homeowner can gain enough knowledge to act as his own general contractor, and this knowledge can save him a considerable amount of money. Acting as your own general contractor can save you between 10% and 30% of the retail price of a general contractor's fees. For an expensive kitchen remodeling job, this can amount to a great deal of money.

Once you decide to involve other people in your job, make a commitment to refine your plans and specifications before starting any work. To show the importance of solid plans, let's look at a sample job and how it might be affected by a lack of proper preparation.

Major Remodeling of a Bathroom

A major bathroom remodeling can be a big undertaking. The work involved can involve a multitude of trades, including any of the following: rough carpentry, trim carpentry, plumbing, electrical, heating, drywall installation, drywall finishing, painting, floor covering, insulation installation, tile installation, and others. Can you do all of these jobs? Only a few homeowners could handle this type of job without professional help.

Since many homeowners don't feel comfortable doing *any* of their own work, let's look at this job through the eyes of a homeowner acting as his own general contractor. If you plan to do portions of your own work, substitute your own labor for the tasks you feel comfortable doing.

First, rip out the existing fixtures and floor covering. This phase of the job doesn't require a lot of skill, but you must be careful not to damage primary systems. You'd have to cut off the water to the plumbing fixtures before removing them, and you'd have to exercise caution when removing light fixtures.

Once the rip-out is complete, get rid of the debris. Have you made plans for removing the debris? If you haven't, here's your first problem.

Now that the rip-out is complete, any needed alterations to the heating or plumbing systems should be done. It's unlikely that there will be a conflict between these first two phases.

After the plumbing and heating rough-ins are done, the electrical work will be done. Again, in a typical job, this shouldn't cause any conflict. However, if you were expanding the size of the bath, or you were remodeling a kitchen, the plumbers, electricians, and heating mechanics might all get in each other's way.

When all the rough-ins are complete and inspected by the local code officer, you're ready to install insulation. There may be no need for additional insulation in some interior remodeling jobs.

After completing any required insulation work and passing inspections, you'll be ready for hanging drywall (Illus. 4-1). This phase should go smoothly. After the drywall is hung, you'll be ready to tape and finish it (Illus. 4-2). This is a dusty job, and it takes some special skills, but there shouldn't be any special problems with this phase.

Now you're ready to paint. What happens when the paint is applied and the finish isn't acceptable? Is it the drywall contractor's fault or the painter's fault? This is a debate that can rage back and forth. There's one way to solve this problem, but you must plan for it in advance:

Insist that the drywall contractor apply a

Illus. 4-1. Attaching furring to walls. Drawing courtesy of United States Gypsum Company

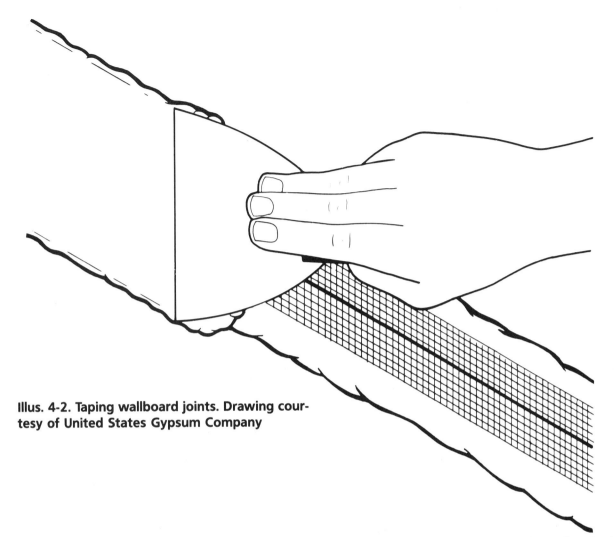

Illus. 4-2. Taping wallboard joints. Drawing courtesy of United States Gypsum Company

coat of primer to the walls before he leaves the job. When the primer is applied, any defects in the finish work will show up. This will pin the fault on the right party. If the walls pass the primer test, move on to the painter, and if the walls don't look good after the painting, hold the painter responsible.

After the painting is done, install the flooring. It isn't unusual for the flooring contractor to mar the finish of new walls, so watch this phase closely. Avoid sending several tradespeople to the job on the same day. If you have more than one trade on the job at a time, you won't know who to blame for damages.

After the flooring is in, you'll be ready for the plumber to set fixtures. Then the heating mechanic can trim out the heating

system, and the electrician can finish the electrical work.

Trim carpentry can be done anytime after the finish flooring is in place, but such carpentry is often done after the mechanical trades are complete.

When everything else is done, the painting contractor will probably have to come back to paint the trim and touch up any places blemished by the other trades.

When all of the work is finished and inspected by the code officers, all that's left is to clean up. Once the cleaning is done, you'll have a fresh, revitalized bathroom.

What could go wrong? Many problems could surface. Suppose the flooring contractor doesn't come as scheduled? This delay will affect your entire schedule. For example, you wouldn't want the plumber to install the toilet and the vanity before the flooring goes in. It's probable that you'd have to reschedule all of the trades following the flooring.

What would happen if one of the tradesmen didn't pass his rough-in inspection? This failure could prevent you from moving ahead with the drywall installation. If you have to postpone the drywall installation, the whole job slows down.

The list of potential problems could go on and on, but you should be getting the idea how loose ends can affect your schedule. These risks escalate when the size of the job is large, as with major kitchen remodeling.

How to Avoid Problems

How you avoid problems will depend largely on the type of job you'll be doing and the number of people involved. First, get all agreements between you and your contractors in writing. The value of well-written contracts is immense. A good contract can protect you and your home, while giving you control over your contractors.

Open communication between the trades is also instrumental for a successful job. Gathering everyone who will be involved on the project together on the job before the work is started can help to eliminate confusion and conflicts before they affect your production schedule.

Material deliveries frequently cause problems. It isn't uncommon for deliveries to be very late. If you have a place to store materials, order early and check each delivery carefully.

If you make any changes in your plans or specifications after the job is started, make sure all your contractors are aware of the changes. While you might not think that changing from a flush-mount medicine cabinet to a recessed medicine cabinet will affect anyone but the carpenters, the mechanical trades could be adversely affected by such a change. The recessed cabinet might conflict with the plumber's vent pipe, the heating mechanic's duct work, or the electrician's wiring plan.

A smooth remodeling job requires good organizational skills and a team effort. If everyone works on his own, oblivious to what others are doing, problems are sure to arise.

Solid Plans, Smooth Jobs

There will more than likely be some changes you won't be able to predict until the job is started, but make an effort to get all the changes made before work begins. No one likes to see a job lose its momentum; you'll be stuck with a job that drags on and on, and the contractors who bid for jobs on a flat-rate fee will lose money.

Planning is probably the most important part of a successful remodeling job. If you plan well in advance and you remain organized at all times, you can better handle the unexpected.

5
Estimating Costs

Cost estimating is a vital part of any remodeling job, and it is a job in itself. Estimating costs for a big remodeling job may seem formidable, but it doesn't have to be. Some people are very well paid to do nothing but estimate costs. Today's technology allows many professionals to rely on computer software for their estimating needs. While it's unlikely that you'll have access to high-tech estimating programs, don't feel helpless, since there are many effective ways for you to develop accurate estimates for labor and material.

If you have the skills to do all of your own work, estimating your costs will be easy. You'll just have to get prices for materials. However, if you can't do all of your work, you'll need some professional help to realize your goals. You must estimate the cost for those professional labor fees.

Since most homeowners need professional help, the following pages will explain the methods used to estimate both material prices and professional labor costs. While any of the methods can produce accurate estimates, combine the methods to assure the most accurate estimates.

Estimating with Contractors' Help

This is the easiest way to figure the cost of your job. Just ask several contractors to give you bids for the job. The contractors will be glad to give you estimates or quotes for the price of labor and materials. This is a simple process, but there are some aspects of this type of estimating that can skew the numbers. If you want accurate figures, follow some basic rules.

Plans

If you'll have contractors do the job for you, a set of plans for what you want done is an absolute necessity. Even if the job is small, you'll want to give a set of plans to each contractor who bids on the work. Without the plans, the contractors can't possibly submit competitive bids.

The plans you give to contractors don't have to be elaborate, but they must detail all important aspects of the job. A rough sketch of what you want done will probably be adequate.

Specifications

Specifications are as important (if not more so) as plans when you work with contractors. When you search for bids, you want all of the contractors to price the same materials and services, which will only be possible with a set of plans and a detailed set of specifications.

Don't list your specifications casually. Don't just say that you want a new toilet, a new lavatory, and new faucets for the lavatory and bathtub. The specifications should include all technical data needed to identify the specific items you want. This information will normally include a model number, style, color, and similar information.

Substitutions

Sometimes contractors make substitutions in materials when they bid on work. If you allow this, it will be impossible to accurately compare the bids you receive. Many contractors use the phrase "or equal" to build in flexibility for substitutions; don't allow such a clause in your quotes or contracts. To obtain accurate estimates, you must be certain that all contractors bid for the job identically.

Contractor's Qualifications

A contractor's qualifications may affect the price you're quoted. Before you finally decide which contractor to select and which price is right, consider the contractor's qualifications.

A building contractor who normally builds new houses may not be well qualified to give accurate price estimates for kitchen remodeling. While this contractor may be very familiar with what it costs to build a house, he may not be experienced with pricing a kitchen remodeling job.

A remodeling contractor who hasn't been in business for very long may not be able to give you accurate quotes. Some contractors will give a low price to get the work, but will they be around to finish the job? A contractor's qualifications could affect the price and service you receive.

If you don't consider the contractor's qualifications, you may find that the estimated price is far too low. Avoid this problem by obtaining numerous bids for the job and comparing them. Avoid very low bids.

Time of Completion

The finish date for a job can affect the price of the work. Some contractors will take a job at a lower price if they can use it as fill-in work. This allows the contractor to have something to work on when other, previously scheduled work doesn't go as planned. For example, if a contractor is scheduled to build an outdoor deck and it rains, what can be done to salvage the day? The contractor could come to your job and work inside.

If you aren't in a hurry to get your job done, this can be a good way to get a low price and a good job. However, if time is of the essence (as it usually is with bathroom and kitchen remodeling), you probably won't be willing to allow the job to drag on for months. Before you accept what appears to be the best bid, establish a finish date.

Time of Day

There are many licensed, insured, reputable contractors who work part-time. These contractors often have full-time jobs during the day and work at their own business at night and on weekends. Such contractors can offer attractive pricing.

If you don't mind having your nights and weekends interrupted with the inconveniences of remodeling, you can save some money by finding part-time contractors. However, if you don't want your leisure hours consumed with noise, dust, and general commotion, you'll probably have to pay more for the work you want done. If you shop for the lowest price, find out why the lowest price is so low.

Quotes & Estimates

What's the difference between *quotes* and *estimates*? Estimates are just that, they don't guarantee a fixed price for a job. Since estimates aren't quotes, you can't hold a contractor to an estimated price. When you try to estimate the cost of your remodeling project, don't base your figures on contractors' estimates; you'll need quotes.

Quotes are guaranteed prices that will neither increase nor decrease. They are usually good for thirty days. Once you make a commitment to sign a contract, the quoted price becomes the contract price, and it shouldn't change. This is the only type of pricing that you can depend on.

Soft Costs

Soft costs are expenses such as permit fees, blueprints, and other fees that aren't related directly to materials and labor. Such costs are sometimes paid by contractors and sometimes paid by homeowners. When you solicit quotes for your job, you need to know if the quotes include all soft costs. Before accepting any quote as the final figure for your job, identify all necessary soft costs and who will pay for them.

Material Take-Offs

Material take-offs are simply lists of materials that will be needed to complete a job. If you plan to estimate your job without the help of contractors, it will be your responsibility to come up with a take-off of the needed materials. These lists are called take-offs because the lists are developed by taking off information about materials from a set of plans. When you look at your plans, you'd see that you need 120 square feet of underlayment to make a take-off for your kitchen floor.

Few homeowners will be able to make accurate take-offs just by using blueprints. For those homeowners working as do-it-yourselfers, this can be a problem. When you hire a plumber to replace your bathroom fixtures, you won't be concerned with how many compression ferrules or supply tubes will be needed; the plumber will take care of all that. However, if you're going to replace your own fixtures, you'll need to estimate the types and amounts of materials you'll need. If you've never replaced plumbing fixtures before, you're likely to make mistakes in your estimates. Estimating the material needs for a complete kitchen redo is even more difficult.

How will you make an accurate material take-off? You could "guesstimate" the needs for the job, but you'll probably wind up with too many of some items and not enough of others. Since it's unlikely that you will be able to produce an accurate list of your needs from blueprints, the best option is to seek professional help.

If your plans will be drawn by a professional, there's a good chance that he'll provide you with a list of materials needed to complete the work. You'll have to pay for the information, but such information should be accurate, and the cost of such a list isn't likely to break your budget.

Other than contractors and professionals, who else can draw plans for accurate take-offs? Seek assistance from material suppliers. Almost any store that sells the materials you need will be willing to help you establish a list of materials based on your plans. Some stores charge for this service, and others provide the service free, as long as you buy your materials from them.

Estimating with Material Suppliers' Help

Estimating costs with the help of material suppliers is a fine way to establish realistic cost projections. Not all take-offs from suppliers will be as accurate as those provided by an architect, but such take-offs will be accurate enough for most needs.

To get a supplier to estimate your material needs and costs, provide the supplier with a set of plans and specifications. Asking a supplier to bid on your job from plans and specs will not necessarily give you a detailed take-off, but it will give you a fixed price to work with. You should get prices from several suppliers and compare them.

Ask the suppliers to break their prices down into phases of work. For example, ask that you be given separate prices for cabinets, countertops, flooring, framing lumber, and so on. If you have several material bids that are broken down this way, you can compare each phase to spot mistakes the suppliers may have made. For example, one supplier may list eight base cabinets where another supplier lists nine. At first you may not know which supplier's take-off is correct, but you'll know that *someone* is wrong.

Once you've obtained and reviewed several estimates for your materials, you'll have a good idea of costs. The only other part of your job to estimate will be soft costs and labor. If you'll be doing the work yourself, estimating the cost of labor won't be important. The soft costs will probably only include permit fees and working drawings, and you might not even need professionally drawn plans.

Cost-Estimating Guides

With the aid of these guides, it's possible to predict the cost for both labor and for materials. There are a number of cost-estimating guides available in bookstores, and most guides provide useful information.

There are drawbacks to estimating books. These quickly become out-of-date. Material prices vary frequently, and estimating books can't foresee these changes. Since the books are written "generically," the figures given might not apply to your particular situation. Use cost-estimating guides in conjunction with the other ways of estimating costs; don't depend on them exclusively.

Good estimating guides provide a way for you to convert their "generic" estimates into regional estimates. Since prices in California are not the same as prices in Florida, the broad-brush estimates must be refined. Multipliers are normally used to compensate for regional differences. These books can be very accurate, and they're an excellent means to evaluate prices given to you by suppliers and contractors.

Cost-estimating manuals usually predict estimates higher than those quoted by most residential contractors. The guides are useful, but don't rely on them as your sole source of information. If you're willing to spend the time to combine all of these estimating methods, you can establish a very accurate cost estimate for your job.

6
Selecting Materials

Selecting materials can be perplexing; it can also be fun. For the average homeowner, differentiating among four different windows (that look the same but have huge differences in cost) can be nearly impossible. Deciding whether to use waferboard or plywood for a subfloor can cause hours of troubled thought. Which type of kitchen faucet will give the best service and appearance for the least amount of money? All of these questions, and more, can arise when you decide which materials to use.

The proper selection of materials can save much money on the overall cost of a large remodeling job. There are times when buying the best materials will pay off, and other times when less expensive materials will get the job done and save you money, without sacrificing appearance or durability.

Picking the proper materials is a skill remodelers often learn from trial-and-error. Learning from experience is effective, but it can be costly. It's unlikely that homeowners will ever do enough remodeling to benefit from the lessons learned the hard way. How can the homeowner avoid costly mistakes? Research is the answer. If you ask enough questions and study enough product literature, you can avoid many pitfalls. You must know which questions to ask.

Subflooring

Subflooring is what's used between the finished floor covering and the floor joists. The subflooring in most remodeling jobs won't have to be replaced, but there are times when it will be, if, for example, the subflooring has been damaged by water or other causes.

The two most common choices for subflooring are plywood and waferboard. If there will only be one layer of subflooring, the material should be of a tongue-and-groove (T&G) type. Some people install two layers of CDX plywood as subflooring, and others install one layer of tongue-and-groove plywood. If only one layer is being used, it's frequently ¾" T&G plywood.

Waferboard is much less expensive than plywood; it's often half the cost. Many professionals install a layer of waferboard and cover it with a thin layer of underlayment. By the time you add up the cost of the two layers and the time it takes to install them, one layer of T&G plywood is often less expensive. However, working with T&G materials in the confined spaces of a bathroom or kitchen can be troublesome. It's easy to build a new house using T&G throughout, but it's difficult to fit it into the tight spaces available in most remodeling jobs.

Since neither kitchen nor bathroom remodeling requires large quantities of subflooring, there won't be a substantial amount of money saved with any method or material. While installing two layers of subflooring may seem like twice as much work as installing one layer of T&G material, under remodeling conditions it really may not be. For most tight-space remodeling jobs, it's easier to install two layers of standard materials than one layer of T&G.

Lumber

Lumber is available in different grades and at different prices. While the studs behind your walls won't be seen after the job is finished, their quality can affect the finished look of your project. Wood that twists and bends will warp the walls and can create defects in the finished wall surface. To avoid problems with lumber, insist on kiln-dried wood. For most applications, a number-2 grade lumber will be your best bet.

Vinyl Flooring

Vinyl flooring (Illus. 6-1) can range dramatically in price. Inexpensive vinyl can be difficult to install; it isn't as flexible as better grades of vinyl. Inexpensive vinyl isn't likely to wear well, and it's prone to more cuts and tears than are better grades.

A moderately priced vinyl flooring should be relatively easy to install, and it should hold up well.

Illus. 6-1. Individual vinyl tiles. Photo courtesy of Azrock Industries, Inc.

Base Cabinets & Wall Cabinets

Cabinets are one of the most expensive elements of kitchen remodeling, and base cabinets account for a big part of this expense. There are sink bases, drawer bases, bases with doors or turntables, bases with pull-out trash receptacles, and so on. These base cabinets are made from many different materials.

Very few cabinets are made of solid wood; most contain some composite materials. True solid-wood cabinets are expensive. Most cabinets will have solid-wood fronts and plywood or particleboard interiors. You'll have to choose between dovetail and butt joints used in cabinet construction; dovetail joints should last longer than butt joints.

When you consider which cabinet doors to buy, decide if you want raised panels, flush doors, doors with finger pulls, or doors meant to accept hardware. This personal choice shouldn't have bearing on the durability of the cabinets.

When you examine drawer bases, test how well the drawers slide in and out. Look for bases that have the drawers mounted on

Illus. 6-2. Decorative laminates. Photo courtesy of Lis King Public Relations

45

good-quality glides that will provide years of trouble-free operation.

Investigate the structural integrity of the base cabinets. Good cabinets have supports in all corners, and the cabinets are firm. Inexpensive cabinets come in a build-it-yourself package (along with screws and little else). Such cabinets are the least desirable, and the least expensive.

Use the same guidelines when you buy wall cabinets. Look for sturdy cabinets that look good and have adjustable shelves.

Avoid bargain cabinets that are sold unfinished. Finishing cabinets isn't easy work, but it is easy to wind up with cabinets that don't match when you attempt to do your own finishing.

Countertops

Don't buy countertops until the base cabinets have been installed. This may slow down the job, but it eliminates much of the risk of buying a countertop that doesn't fit. You usually won't be able to return countertops, so it's important to get the right top to begin with.

If you buy your cabinets and counters from a custom cabinet company, you won't have to worry about measurements; a company representative will measure your kitchen and arrive at the proper sizes. However, if you deal with a general supplier, you may have to take measurements for your own countertop. If you have to do this, have the supplier explain to you exactly how to make the measurements for the type of countertop you'll be ordering.

Good, durable countertops are not extremely expensive, and they're available in a number of different colors and designs. Browse through samples at your building supplier to see all the options (Illus. 6-2). Expensive, specialty counters are not usually justified in average kitchens, but there are many high-cost tops available.

Kitchen Sinks

Kitchen sinks can vary greatly in cost. Most modern kitchens are equipped with double-bowl stainless-steel sinks. Some kitchens have enamel-over-cast-iron sinks, and some sinks have single bowls or double bowls with specialty bowls. A simple stainless-steel sink, with two bowls, is adequate for most kitchens.

While all stainless-steel sinks may look alike, there are differences. Some sinks are coated to reduce the noise made by water running into them. This invisible sound-proofing, may be worthwhile, although it costs extra. The big difference between stainless-steel sinks is the gauge of the metal. Some sinks are so flimsy that a garbage disposer will pull the bowl downward. Look for a sink that doesn't dimple in and pop out when you press on the drain hole. A 20-gauge sink is stronger than a 22-gauge sink.

Lavatories

Lavatories fluctuate wildly in price. A simple wall-hung lavatory (Illus. 6-3) will be inexpensive, but a good double-bowl lavatory (Illus. 6-4) will cost much more. You can buy a plastic lavatory, a china lavatory, or an enamel-over-cast-iron lavatory. China lavatories are the most common, and they hold up well.

Toilets

There are many very expensive toilets available, but a standard two-piece toilet will do fine, and is relatively inexpensive. One-piece toilets look good, but they don't work any better than do two-piece toilets. To go beyond the basics is to pay for aesthetics, neither for function nor durability.

Bathtubs

Bathtubs can be made from plastic, fiberglass, enamel-over-cast-iron, or enameled steel. Any of these tubs can provide years of dependable service, but prices can differ considerably. A cast-iron bathtub can be very expensive, while a steel tub (that looks about the same) can cost a fraction of that. With either of these two types of tubs, dropping a hard or sharp object in them can result in cracked enamel and an eventual need for repairs. Both of these tubs will be much colder to sit in than a plastic or fiberglass tub would be.

Fiberglass has become the most common material for bathtubs. These tubs are generally durable and well accepted. They're available as sectional units that allow for a one-piece look made from modular units.

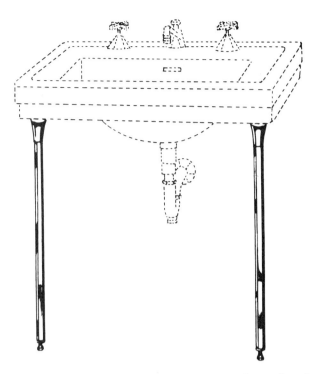

Illus. 6-3. A wall-hung lavatory with optional legs. Drawing printed with permission of Nu-Tone, Inc., Cincinnati, Ohio 45227

Illus. 6-4. Double-bowl vanity with tilt-out trays.
Photo courtesy of Decora'

This can be very useful to the remodeler who can't get a standard one-piece tub-shower combination into the house. These units are, of course, available without the surrounding walls, at a lower price.

Showers

Most showers installed today are made of fiberglass. Like modular tubs, showers are available as modular units. Some modulars give the appearance of a one-piece unit, and others use a shower base that's surrounded by walls of a different material. Typically, showers cost more than the tub-shower combinations.

Light Fixtures

You can spend a little or a lot for light fixtures and not really be able to see much difference. Recessed light fixtures are inexpensive, but they only provide limited illumination.

Bar lights for the bathroom are inexpensive, and the same type of light in an oak finish will cost slightly more, giving you an attractive bar light with three large light bulbs for a very reasonable price.

Track lighting is very popular, and it can give plenty of illumination in different directions. Track lighting can be especially attractive and useful in a kitchen. Since track lighting is comprised of component parts, the price will vary with the style you select and the number of housings installed on the track. Track lighting is a very affordable way to get good lighting.

Windows

Windows can be especially confusing and bothersome to evaluate, since many types and styles of windows are available (see the color photo on page 66). To eliminate some

confusion you can read literature about the products.

The energy efficiency of windows is rated in terms of "U-value." The lower U-value, the better and more efficient the window is. A window with a U-value of 4 would be more energy-efficient than a window with a U-value of 5.

Casement windows are generally considered to be some of the most energy-efficient types of windows. Casement windows crank open and allow a full flow of ventilation.

Metal-frame windows tend to sweat or condensate. This moisture can cause damage to surrounding wood areas, and the dripping and mold can be annoying to look at.

Wood windows provide good insulation and don't amplify sounds as greatly as metal windows do, but wood windows require routine maintenance.

Vinyl windows and vinyl-clad wood windows eliminate the need for painting. These maintenance-free windows are favored by many homeowners.

Other window options include gas-filled windows, low-E glass, glass that blocks UV rays, and so on. There are so many possibilities that you must study brochures from numerous manufacturers to determine which features matter to you.

Trim

The trim materials you install (Illustrations 6-5, 6-6) will affect the finished look of your new kitchen or bathroom. There are several choices available, but the two basic types of trim are "finger-joint" and "clear." Finger-joint trim is less expensive than clear trim, but it isn't suitable for staining. If you paint your trim, finger-joint is fine. When you stain the trim, be sure it's clear trim or what is called "stain-grade" trim.

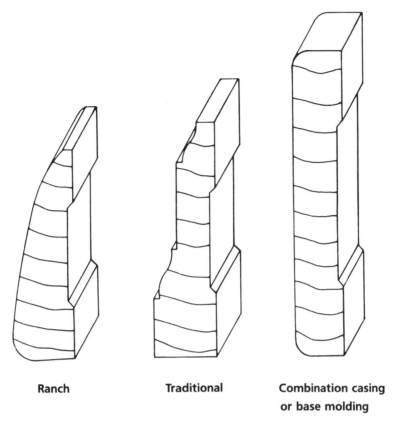

Ranch   Traditional   Combination casing
                                    or base molding

Illus. 6-5. Types of casing material. Drawing courtesy of USDA Forest Service

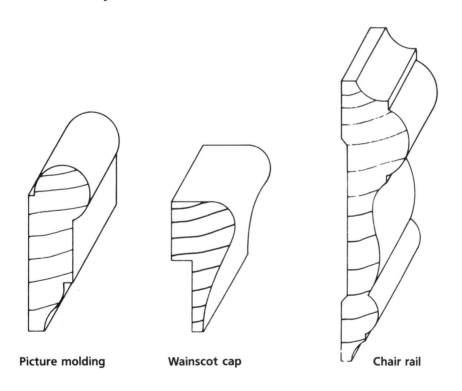

Picture molding   Wainscot cap   Chair rail

Illus. 6-6. Wall moldings. Drawing courtesy of USDA Forest Service

49

Colonial-style baseboards and casing are generally considered good grades of standard trim. Clam-type baseboards are less expensive, and they're typically associated with low-quality construction. Use regular boards for trim to achieve a rustic look.

Choosing the Right Materials

The key to choosing the right materials is research. Educate yourself with product literature and books as an effective way to make sound purchasing decisions. If you don't understand what you're reading, ask professionals for their interpretations and opinions. If you budget yourself adequate time to select your materials, you should be able both to save money and to get good materials.

7
Shopping for the Best Price for Materials

Shopping for the best price for materials won't be difficult once you know which materials you need and want. Once you have a detailed list of material specifications, all that should be necessary is to circulate the list among suppliers and wait for the best price. However, in reality, you'll have to exert some energy to find the best bargains.

I once shopped for materials from four different suppliers for the construction of a new house. I submitted identical plans and specifications to the four suppliers and asked for detailed quotes. When all the quotes were in, there was quite a spread from the lowest to the highest bid.

When I saw this range I looked for errors in the bid sheets, but I found none. Next, I compared the bids on an item-by-item basis. In some cases substitutes were used for the materials I had originally requested, but for the most part the difference was simply in the prices. If this situation can happen to me, a professional contractor who buys materials on a daily basis, imagine how you, a homeowner, might be treated.

Aggressive shopping can save a great deal of money on a kitchen or bathroom remodeling job. There's a point when running from store to store is not cost-effective, but sometimes it pays to deal with more than one supplier. Many people feel that they'll get the best deal by purchasing all of their materials from the same vendor. While this should be true, it isn't always the case.

Circulate Your Plans & Specifications

First, circulate your plans and specifications. If you have a detailed takeoff of the materials you want priced, the takeoff is all you need to distribute. Send bid-request packages to several suppliers. If your job is a big one, it may pay to send bid packages to suppliers in other cities or states. It is amazing how prices can vary from city to city and from state to state.

If you do shop for materials from distant suppliers, keep shipping costs in mind; they may outweigh any price advantage. Consider the disadvantages of distant suppliers in terms of product assistance and returns on damaged or improperly shipped items.

Call each supplier to whom you'll send a bid package, and request the name of an appropriate person to whom you'll address the package. Your package might get shoved aside and neglected if it's not specifically addressed to someone.

After the bid packages have had time to arrive at the various suppliers, call each supplier and speak with your contact person. Confirm the delivery of your package and ask if there are any questions on the items you want priced. Inform the contact person not to make substitutions unless absolutely necessary, and if substitutions must be made, have the contact tell the estimator to note the changes in red ink. Insist that the bid be prepared in phases. For example, you might have the following phases for a bathroom job: framing materials, wall coverings, plumbing fixtures, paint, cabinets, light fixtures, and so on. Having your bids broken down into distinct categories will make your overall evaluations easier.

Review the Quotes

Go over the quotes when you have plenty of time and you won't be disturbed. Work at a large table to allow you to lay all quotes next to each other for a quick, one-to-one comparison.

If all of your quotes come back broken down into the proper phases, consider yourself lucky. Suppliers don't like to break down their bids, and they know that you're more likely to spot high prices if you can compare prices side-by-side. Most suppliers prefer to give a lump-sum figure at the end of a computer-generated printout. When the quotes aren't broken down properly, you'll have to work a little harder to determine the real essence of the bid.

Look at the price of a 2×4 stud from each supplier. Check each supplier's price (per square yard) for your floor covering. Undoubtedly there will be variations among these items. While it's senseless to run all over town buying studs from one supplier, nails from another, and plywood from yet another, it does make sense to shop in phases.

Not all suppliers get the same discounts on all materials. One supplier may have a great price on cabinets and a terrible price on floor coverings. Buy flooring from one store and cabinets from another.

The Bottom Line

The bottom line can be quite deceiving. If you look at four bids, it will be easy to see which vendor offers the lowest overall price, but his bid isn't necessarily the lowest price possible for the materials you need.

Not all suppliers can sell the same products for the same price and make a profit, even if they wanted to. There are, of course, some items that can be bought for less money from competitive suppliers.

By shopping for bids in phases, you'll find the best prices available. You might have to deal with six different suppliers to save the most money, but you won't lose much time in doing so. There's nothing wrong with dealing with multiple suppliers.

What's Included?

What's included in each of the bids? Have all the suppliers included sales tax? This one item can make a sizable difference. The supplier who's included the tax in the bid will appear to be priced higher than the bids from suppliers who didn't include the tax; this is a common situation.

Will the suppliers include delivery for the prices quoted? Delivery may not be particularly important if you have your own truck and you're only buying a few items, but if you are ordering for your whole job, delivery can be an expensive problem. Most suppliers will include free delivery within a certain distance of their warehouse. Determine the price of delivery before you make a commitment to a supplier.

Are the items you want normally in stock? If a supplier quotes a price for materials that aren't normally in stock, you may be faced with delays and extra, hidden costs. When the supplier doesn't stock an item, you may have to pay for the shipping charges to have the item delivered to the supplier. It's unlikely that the supplier will reveal this expense in a competitive bid.

Once You Have Preliminary Prices

Once you have preliminary prices, you can begin the *real* negotiations. Most suppliers give professional contractors a discount on the price of materials. This discount is rarely offered to homeowners. However, if the suppliers can sell to contractors for less, they can also sell to you for less, but you'll have to convince them to do so.

Let's assume that you've gone over all of your bids and one supplier has offered you the best prices on everything except floor coverings and plumbing fixtures. You could buy these last items from other suppliers to get your best price, or you could try negotiating with the same supplier who offered the best prices for all of the other items.

If you want to deal with just one supplier, take the other bids with you and go in for a personal visit with the supplier's representative. Explain that you'd like to buy all of your materials from one store, but you can't justify the extra expense for the flooring and plumbing fixtures just for the sake of convenience. Ask the sales representative if anything can be done to lower the prices of the two "overpriced" items.

If the sales representative feels the entire order may be in jeopardy, there's a good chance that the sales manager will authorize a lower price on the flooring and plumbing fixtures. Remember, they probably already have a profit cushion built into the entire order. With a little persuasive negotiating, you can probably get the best price and only have to deal with one vendor.

It may also be possible to negotiate for at least a portion of the discount normally offered to contractors. Many contractors use their credit to finance their purchases for thirty days. Since you will most likely be paying in full upon delivery, use these payment terms as leverage. Impress upon the sales manager that there won't be any risk in collecting a bad account, and that the store won't really lose money by giving you the same discount offered to professionals.

There are many ways to drive a hard bargain if you're willing to spend the time and effort to do it. Suppliers don't want to see their competition get your business, and this gives you an edge. You don't really care where the material comes from, so you can shop until you get the deal you want.

Once you have your materials secured for a good price, you may need to find and hire some subcontractors to help you get the job done.

8
Subcontractors

What do you know about subcontractors? Are you aware that the carpenter you hire to do framing work may have neither the skills nor the desire to do trim work? Who hangs and sets the cabinets in the kitchen? Will a plumber install a dishwasher or will an electrician? Do plumbing-and-heating companies deal with duct work and furnaces?

If you act as your own general contractor, you must know which types of subcontractors will be needed for different phases of your job. Even small remodeling jobs can involve many different members of the building trades.

Once you get your job started, the issue of subcontractors will probably confuse you.

Today's conditions have changed the way the building trades work. It used to be that a carpenter could and would do almost any type of work that involved wood. Whether the job was making cabinets, building a barn, or hanging a door, almost any carpenter could handle the job. This isn't the case today, when carpenters (and other tradespeople) are often highly specialized.

Since you will be searching for the best talent for your job, you must know which specialists to seek. Being unaware of specialization trends can create confusion and frustration. Imagine going through the telephone directory calling plumbers to help remodel your kitchen. How would you respond if you were turned down by the first five plumbers you called?

It's hard to believe a plumber would re-fuse remodeling work, but some will. If the plumbing company deals only in repair and service work, it won't be equipped to handle remodeling. If the company does only commercial work, it won't be able to do residential work. Plumbers who specialize in new construction will have no interest in a dirty remodeling job. Let's look at each trade you may need. Chapter 9 will show you how to properly select subcontractors.

Debris Contractors

Most homeowners never think about hiring debris contractors until such material begins to pile up. The amount of trash that can accumulate during remodeling is surprising. There will be old lumber, flooring, fixtures, cardboard, and many other materials that must be discarded. This removal can't be reasonably done by using the trunk of your car. Who'll get rid of the rubbish? This question has become harder to answer with new rules at landfills and mandatory recycling in some places.

Debris contractors may haul the unwanted material away in the bed of a truck or in a storage container. Most remodeling contractors rent a trash container that's placed on the job site. When the container is full, the container is removed, emptied, and returned. You'll undoubtedly need to make some arrangements for the removal of debris.

Rough Carpenters

Rough carpenters usually do framing. If you were building a new house, you might have a crew of rough carpenters erect the shell of the home. In the case of remodeling, you might find one carpenter to do all the work involved, or you may have to look for different types of carpenters. If you won't be expanding your kitchen or bathroom, you won't have much need for rough carpenters.

Trim Carpenters

Trim carpenters hang doors, install baseboard trim, install window casing, and so forth. These carpenters are good with detail work, and while many of them work slowly, they often work to perfection. Some (but not all) trim carpenters will install cabinets.

Cabinet Installers

Cabinet installers, who may do nothing but install cabinets, frequently work for companies that sell cabinets. If you search for a subcontractor to install your cabinets, start your search by asking the cabinet supplier for referrals.

Insulation Contractors

Insulation contractors aren't always needed for kitchen or bathroom remodeling jobs. However, if the remodeling job involves building an addition onto the home, an insulation contractor may be needed. Most insulation contractors have separate crews for different types of work. If you call an insulation company, it should have a crew organized to do the work you request.

Drywall Hangers

On small jobs, drywall hangers often do the finishing work. However, on large jobs it's not uncommon for one subcontractor to hang the drywall and for another to finish the drywall for paint.

Drywall Finishers

Drywall finishers usually have the skills needed to hang wallboard, but their time is more valuable finishing drywall than it is hanging it. It's unusual to use separate contractors to hang and finish drywall on a small job, but it may be to your advantage. People who spend every day finishing walls and ceilings are usually going to be better at it than people who spend half their time hanging drywall.

Wallpaper Hangers

You could hang wallpaper by yourself (Illustrations 8-1, 8-2, 8-3, 8-4), but wallpaper hangers are specialists. Using professional hangers should result in a uniform and appealing job. If you're inexperienced working with wallpaper, it's easy to mismatch patterns and seams.

Painters

Anyone can paint walls and ceilings, but professional painters tend to do a much better job than the layman. The painter has many tricks of the trade, and your job will benefit from his expertise.

Electricians

Some electricians do only commercial work, while others do only repair work. Neither of these electricians will be the best choice for a remodeling job. What you need is an electrician who does residential work, and preferably one who does remodeling work. There are substantial differences between wiring a new house and wiring a remodeling job. Expend the extra effort to find an electrician who has remodeling experience.

55

Illus. 8-1. Preparing a wall surface for wallpaper. Drawing courtesy of Lis King Public Relations

Illus. 8-2. Applying wallpaper. Drawing courtesy of Lis King Public Relations

Illus. 8-3. Seaming wallpaper. Drawing courtesy of Lis King Public Relations

Heating Mechanics

If you won't be adding space or relocating existing heating units, you probably won't need heating mechanics, but if you do need them, look for those who are experienced in residential remodeling. Heating mechanics specialize in a way that's similar to electricians and plumbers.

Plumbers

Plumbers specialize in many types of work, some specialize in sewer cleaning, well systems, water-conditioning systems, new construction, commercial work, residential work, repair work, remodeling, water-service and sewer installations, and so on. Find a plumber who's expert at residential remodeling.

Flooring Installers

Flooring installers are often found in or through the stores that sell floor covering. The flooring installer who replaces carpeting may not install vinyl flooring. While most flooring installers will work with any type of carpet or vinyl, be sure that you get someone experienced in the type of work you require.

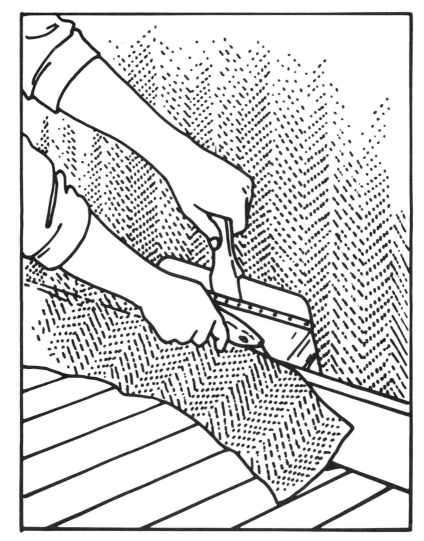

Illus. 8-4. Trimming wallpaper. Drawing courtesy of Lis King Public Relations

Tile Contractors

If you want tile installed, you may need tile contractors, who can be found in telephone directories, or through the store where you bought your tile.

Siding Contractors

If you add space to your home, or install new windows, you may need siding contractors. Many carpenters will work with siding, but there are companies that specialize in siding.

Roofers

It's unlikely that you'll need roofers for an average kitchen or bath remodeling, but if you'll be installing skylights, bay windows, or adding space, you might. Most carpenters are willing to do minor roofing jobs, but if the work is extensive, it may be less expensive to deal directly with a roofer.

9
Selecting Subcontractors

It's likely that you'll need at least a few subcontractors when you remodel your kitchen or bathroom. Selecting these subcontractors is a job in itself. Choosing the wrong people could turn your dream kitchen into a nightmare. If you hire a general contractor to handle the entire job for you, the burden of choosing subcontractors will be his. Exercise prudence when picking a general contractor. Unless you do all aspects of the job yourself, you'll have to deal with contractors.

Finding and selecting the right subcontractors isn't easy, and I speak from experience. At one point in my career I was building nearly sixty homes per year, and I required much help. I had some tradespeople on my payroll, but most of the labor was provided by subcontractors. In a single year, I dealt with more than 120 subcontractors and vendors.

I started in construction as a plumbing subcontractor. As my experience and business grew, I moved into remodeling and building; it was then that I became a general contractor. Having been a subcontractor and having worked around other subcontractors, I had more experience with them than do most new general contractors. Even with this experience, finding, choosing, and keeping the best subcontractors was a chore, and it still is.

If a professional general contractor (like me) has to continue to work at finding and selecting good subs, a homeowner should not underrate the task at hand.

This chapter will show you how to find and select the best subcontractors. You'll learn how to qualify the candidates for the type of work you need done, and you'll see some of the potential problems.

Where to Find Subcontractors

The advertising pages of your local telephone directory would be a logical place to start. Contractors listed there have been established in business for at least a little while, and they're easy to locate.

Newspapers

Local newspapers are another good place to look for subcontractors. Advertising rates in telephone directories are steep, and some good contractors have nothing more than a line listing there. Such contractors prefer to spend their advertising budget selectively, and the newspaper is one of the places they may use to advertise to the public.

Friends

Ask your friends if they know of any reputable contractors. It is hard to beat trusted word-of-mouth referrals when searching for good contractors.

Signs

Drive around your neighborhood, and look for signs that indicate that remodelers are working in your area. When doing a job, many contractors display signs with their company names and phone numbers. Finding contractors in this way shows you that they're working, and that you'll probably be able to inspect their work.

Qualities to Seek in a Subcontractor

There are some attributes to seek.

Licensed

Any contractor you hire should be licensed to conduct business. Many trades, such as plumbing, heating, and electrical trades, require special licensing. For example, a plumbing contractor should hold a master plumber's license. Having a journeyman plumbing license is not sufficient for most plumbing contracting.

Check with your local building-code and licensing authorities to determine which licenses are required for which types of work. Don't hire contractors who aren't properly licensed.

Insured

Any contractor you consider for your job should be properly insured. Insurance for contractors is expensive, and many contractors don't have it. Hiring an uninsured contractor is very risky.

Verify a contractor's insurance with the agency issuing the insurance policy; don't take the contractor's word for it. If you review a contractor's certificate of insurance examine the dates carefully; the policy may have expired.

Experienced

Experience in remodeling is vital to a successful job. It's easy for contractors to say they have years of experience with remodeling; make them prove it. Contractors who work with new construction are not always qualified remodelers. There are significant differences between remodeling and new work.

References

Contractors should prove their experience in remodeling. Check their references; and insist on at least five references. Devious contractors will expect you to ask for three references, and they may have three friends or relatives prepared to pose as references. By asking for five references, you may be able to catch such contractors off guard. Ideally, you should visit jobs the contractors are doing to see that the references you've been given are real.

Stability

Business stability in remodeling and contracting can be difficult to maintain. Swings in the economy can bankrupt a company that was once thriving. Some businesses that present a strong public image can be on the verge of collapse. When you entrust your money and your home to contractors, you're entitled to know that your trust isn't misplaced. Find out as much as you can about the contractor and the stability of his business.

How to Verify Information Given by Subcontractors

A subcontractor's insurance information can be verified by calling the insurance agency providing his coverage. References can be called, but they should be visited, whenever possible. Licensing information can be verified with the licensing agencies in your area. Experience is difficult to verify, but checking references will provide some security.

If the contractor will give permission for you to talk with material suppliers, the suppliers can tell you much about the stability of the contractor's business. Speaking with the contractor's bank personnel is another way to check for business stability.

Many contractors belong to professional organizations that may be willing to provide background information. Credit reports on the contractors can be helpful, but few subcontractors will provide homeowners with the same verifications they'll offer a professional general contractor.

Getting answers to all of your questions won't be easy. Many subcontractors will consider your requests unusual and to be more trouble than your business is worth. Since most homeowners ask contractors very few questions, the few who do face an uphill battle. While you can't expect to be completely safe when working with subcontractors, play it safe and learn as much as possible about the contractors.

Choose Back-Up Subcontractors

When you begin selecting subs, choose back-up subcontractors right from the start. Invariably, there are times when the subcontractors you want to do the job won't work out. Sometimes they'll suffer injuries and be unable to perform the work. There will be occasions when the contractors are behind schedule and can't get to your job when they're supposed to. Some contractors may simply disappear. It's better that this should happen before work starts, rather than after. There are dozens of good reasons for selecting back-up contractors.

Wise professionals always have at least three subcontractors for each phase of work. Having three plumbers chosen in advance will prevent a catastrophe. Don't put all your trust in one subcontractor.

When you sort through potential contractors, give them ratings. For example, when considering drywall contractors, establish a first, second, and third choice for your job. This type of planning may allow you to avoid trouble once the job is started.

Beware of Sales Hype

Some contractors are better at selling their services than providing them. Screen all contractors carefully to avoid "camouflaged" salespeople. The best salespeople won't appear to be selling you anything. True sales professionals can make you buy products and services you don't need and don't want. Learning this from experience can be very costly.

Protect yourself from impulse buying by refusing to make an on-the-spot decision. If you're told that if you don't act immediately the price will go up, look for another contractor. If you're told you should remodel your bathroom and kitchen at the same time, think over the proposition. There's a good chance that you could save money by having both jobs done simultaneously, but if your bathroom doesn't need to be remodeled, you'll waste your money.

Satisfaction

To be satisfied with a completed job, you'll need dependable, reputable, experienced subcontractors. Spend enough time selecting them to ensure satisfaction. The wrong contractors can turn your job into a fiasco; the right contractors can make difficult work look easy.

10
Getting the Best Price from Contractors

The prices contractors quote for similar work can vary greatly. It wouldn't be unusual to find a great range of hourly rates for plumbers, and the same could be said for any subcontractors. Even if the difference between hourly rates is small, the cost over the course of the job can really add up.

Here's an example showing how the hourly rates used by two plumbers when estimating a bathroom remodeling job might affect your costs. One plumber's labor costs $25/hour, and the other prices his labor at $35/hour. Both plumbers estimate the same amount of time for the work required.

When the plumbers estimate the time they'll devote to removing existing fixtures, they figure five hours plus travel time and miscellaneous time. To round it off, they both consider the rip-out to be worth eight hours of their time.

When figuring the labor for installing new fixtures, both plumbers arrive at an estimate of an additional eight hours. Allowing for inspections, handling material acquisitions and other administrative duties are billed as an additional eight hours.

Using broad-brush estimating techniques, both plumbers have arrived at estimates of twenty-four hours for their labor. The higher estimate is $840 and the lower estimate is $600.

Assume that the total cost for all labor used to remodel a bathroom will be $4,000.

If you could shave 30% off that labor figure, you'd save $1,200. Is it possible to save this much money and still get a good job? It's possible, but it will require some additional effort on your part.

Finding the best prices for labor takes patience and persistence. Contractors won't work for free, but they may be willing to offer discounts, if you know how to bargain. There are ways to convince contractors to give you a lower price for the privilege of getting your job.

Fill-In Work

All contractors love fill-in work, which is work they can do when circumstances prohibit them from doing regularly scheduled work. If it's raining, and a carpenter can't work outside, having a fill-in job doing inside work is a welcome pleasure. If a delivery is mixed up on one job and brings a crew to a halt, the contractor won't lose much money if his crew can be sent to work on a fill-in job.

Since fill-in jobs are valuable to contractors, you can often negotiate for a lower price if you're willing to allow your job to be a fill-in job. This works well with some types of home improvements, but it usually isn't a good idea with kitchen remodeling. If you have more than one bathroom, consider having your additional bathroom remodeled on a fill-in basis, but be prepared to do without the use of that bathroom for an extended period.

Due to the nature of fill-in jobs, they don't get finished quickly. If you're willing to allow your job to remain unfinished for weeks, or perhaps months, you'll be in a good position to bargain for a lower price. If you need the work completed in a timely fashion, don't consider using a "fill-in."

Reference Jobs

A job that can be used as a reference for future customers isn't always easy for contractors to obtain. If homeowners are willing to show completed jobs to prospective customers, contractors can close more sales.

If you're willing to allow contractors to use your job as a reference, you should receive something for the inconvenience, perhaps a lower price for the work being done.

If you negotiate with contractors to use your house as an example of their work, you gain in two ways. First, you'll get a lower price for the services you receive. Second, since the job will be used to display the contractors' talents, you'll reap the benefits of the best job the contractors can do.

Using your home as a showplace is a very effective way to negotiate for a better price and sometimes for better materials. The contractors will be showing the job to future customers, and the former will want their new customers to be favorably impressed. If you do agree to such an arrangement, establish the terms in writing. Dictate how much notice you will be given prior to showings, how long your job will be used as a reference, and how many showings will be allowed per week.

New Companies

New companies are frequently hungry for business and references. Dealing with the right new companies can save you a considerable amount of money. Choose your contractors carefully. Many of these new business owners are not new to their business, only to owning it. The contractors could have twenty years of experience doing their job and have only been in business for a month.

There are risks when you deal with fledgling companies, but there are also rewards. If the contractors are honest and experienced, you can get better service than you might from a large, established company, and the price will almost always be less.

Should you gamble on using a new company, first do your homework. Make sure the business is insured and licensed. While there may not be much to investigate, investigate everything you can about the company and its owner.

Negotiate!

Negotiate with contractors! If you haggle over other purchases, why not negotiate for a better price from contractors? In many cases the full price of a major remodeling job is more than the cost of an average new car, so certainly there's enough money involved to be worth the effort of bargaining. Many homeowners never question the prices given by contractors. They either look elsewhere for a lower price or accept the price they're given.

If you find a perfect contractor, don't let his high bid alienate you. Good contractors are hard to find, and when you do find one, you should make an effort to work out a viable deal. Contractors aren't different from other business owners, they're willing to consider offers and to negotiate.

I've been involved in construction for nearly twenty years, many of those years as a contractor, and I've rarely had homeowners bargain with me. As a subcontractor, I have had plenty of general contractors bargain for better prices, but few homeowners ever do.

Very few contractors show all their cards on the initial bid; they bid jobs expecting to negotiate. When homeowners accept the bid as is, the contractors pocket some extra profits. If homeowners look at the prices and continue to search for other, lower-priced contractors, the contractors with the padded bids will lose out.

While many good contractors don't inflate their prices enormously, most do build in a buffer of at least 5%. It isn't unusual for contractors to inflate their prices by 10%. Knowing this, you should try to squeeze that price cushion out of the contractors. Saving 5% on an expensive kitchen job means big savings, sometimes enough to pay for a new microwave oven or a dishwasher.

Remodel with the Seasons

There are certain times of the year when contractors have less work than they'd like to have. If you can arrange to have your job done during an off-season, many contractors will reward you with a lower price. There are several good times of the year for you to take advantage of special prices and incentives. Let's look at each month to establish the best buying times.

January

January is an excellent time to schedule remodeling work. Many homeowners are still paying bills from the holiday season. In most regions, January weather isn't conducive to construction. January is a good time to save some money on remodeling.

February

February is often cold and dreary, making it an excellent time to offer contractors inside work. However, February is also the month when many contractors gear up for the spring rush, so they might not be quite as flexible as they had been in January.

March

The odds favor contractors this month. People who have been depressed through the winter see a glimmer of hope for warm, sunny days, and they're more likely to have a positive outlook. This change in attitude often results in consumer purchases: home improvements, houses, cars, and so on. Avoid remodeling in March.

April–June

These are months to avoid. By April, people are sure summer is getting closer, and they're ready to go on spending sprees. This isn't a good time to look for bargains in home improvements. Spring is the worst season to look for home-improvement values.

July–August

July and August can offer some opportunities for bargain hunters. Many people vacation during these two months, resulting in less work for contractors. The summer heat can also make contractors look for inside, air-conditioned work. If July isn't the best month for home-improvement values, it's better than the spring months.

During August, many parents are readying their children for school or college. The costs and duties of "back to school" days prevent some people from pursuing remodeling. This lack of interest in remodeling may work to your advantage.

September

This isn't a good month for discount-remodeling prices. This is when many people decide to remodel before winter, so avoid shopping in September.

October

October is worse than September for bar-

(Continued on page 81)

An elegant bathroom with a pedestal lavatory. Photo courtesy of Benjamin Moore & Co.

Casement window. Photo courtesy of Marvin Windows and Doors

Cutaway views of good-quality windows. Photo courtesy of Marvin Windows and Doors

Lavatory in a vanity, with Mellowtones tile on the walls and floor. Photo courtesy of American Olean Tile Company

A tile floor in a kitchen. Tile manufactured by The Tileworks, Des Moines, IA

Sheet vinyl in a kitchen. Photo courtesy of Mannington Resilient Floors

Sheet vinyl in a kitchen. Photo courtesy of Mannington Resilient Floors

Tiled counter, back-splash, and floor. Photo courtesy of American Olean Tile Company

A well-appointed kitchen. Photo courtesy of Wood-Mode, Inc.

Tiled walls in a kitchen. Photo courtesy of American Olean Tile Company

A pull-out cutting block. Photo courtesy of Wood-Mode, Inc.

A pull-out caddy. Photo courtesy of Wood-Mode, Inc.

A space-saving cabinet accessory. Photo courtesy of Wood-Mode, Inc.

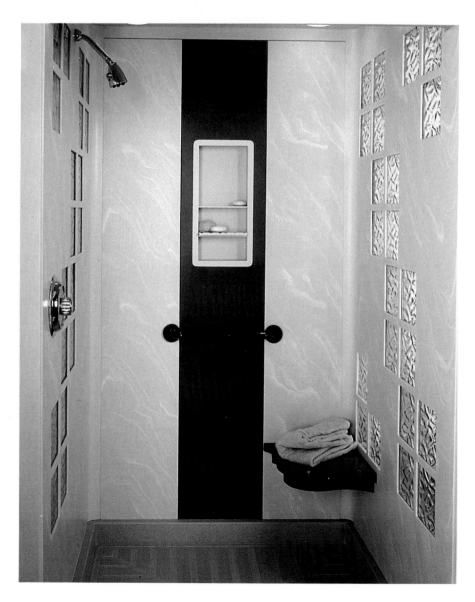

Corian™ shower surround. Photo courtesy of Du Pont

Carriage House, "Vintage" & "Cathedral" doors, "Walden" stain on cherry. Photo courtesy of Plain 'n Fancy Custom Cabinetry

Carriage House, "Vintage II" doors, white enamel on birch. Photo courtesy of Plain 'n Fancy Custom Cabinetry

"Vintage" and "Cathedral" doors, "Heirloom" stain on cherry. Photo courtesy of Plain 'n Fancy Custom Cabinetry

"Arias II," "Contempo II" doors, natural and white laminate on oak. Photo courtesy of Plain 'n Fancy Custom Cabinetry

"Shaker II" door, burnished stain on cherry. Photo courtesy of Plain 'n Fancy Custom Cabinetry

Weatherburne, "Pine Frost," "Cambridge" door, beaded inset. Photo courtesy of Plain 'n Fancy Custom Cabinetry

Doubleton door, "Lynford" stain on oak. Photo courtesy of Plain 'n Fancy Custom Cabinetry

"Strata II" doors, natural oak. Photo courtesy of Plain 'n Fancy Custom Cabinetry

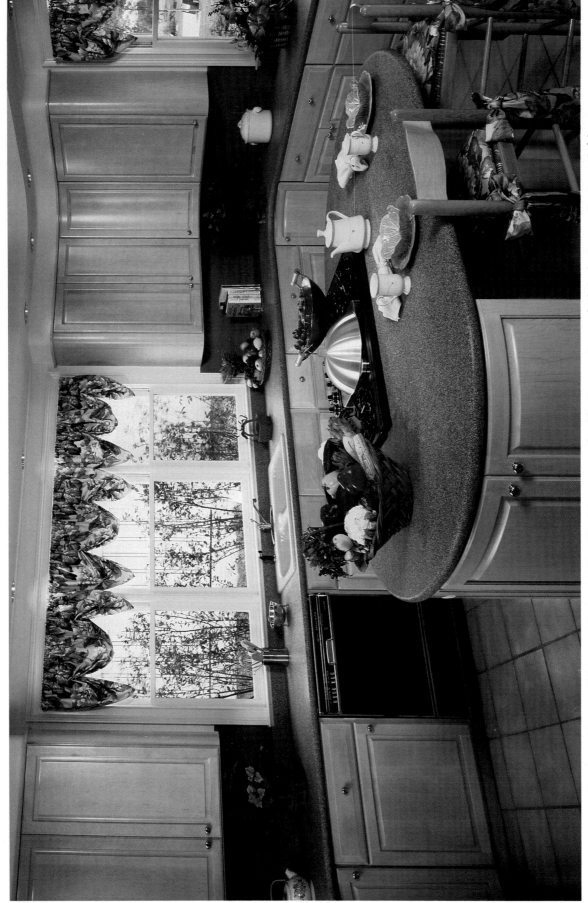

Carriage House, "Vintage II" door, "Pearl" stain on maple. Photo courtesy of Plain 'n Fancy Custom Cabinetry

gain hunting. People are rushing about to get their homes in order before the holidays, and contractors have no shortage of work during these times.

November

By the middle of the month, the remodeling market becomes a buyer's market. Most people don't want contractors in their homes during Thanksgiving, and this means lower prices for the homeowners.

December

December is an excellent month for low remodeling prices. Most people don't contemplate remodeling between Thanksgiving and Christmas, so there's an enormous opportunity to save money. Contractors often want extra money for Christmas.

A creative homeowner can find many ways to persuade contractors to offer lower prices. You should be able to save substantial money on your job by strategic shopping and negotiating.

11
Permits & Building-Code Compliance

All homeowners involved with remodeling should be aware of these two items. If you'll be doing your own remodeling, these aspects are of the utmost importance. When you hire a general contractor to do the job for you, you shouldn't have to worry about building-code compliance and permits, but if you're smart, learn (at least in general terms) what should and shouldn't be done.

Unfortunately, not all contractors play by the rules. Some contractors avoid getting permits for their jobs in order to keep the price of the work lower. A few contractors are unable to get permits, because they aren't licensed, and therefore never inform their customers of a need for permits and inspections. Don't perform work that requires a permit and inspection without first obtaining proper authorization.

Any work that doesn't comply with code requirements may have to be torn out and redone. If you're unlucky enough to hire a bad contractor, you might pay for the contractor's expensive mistakes.

Almost every town, city, and county has a code-enforcement office and official code inspectors. The inspectors are employed to protect the citizens of the jurisdiction, including you. While arranging for code inspections may not be something you want to do, it may be required by law in your area, and the inspection may protect you from many hazards.

Must All Work Be Inspected?

Not all work requires a permit or an inspection, but much of the remodeling work in kitchens and bathrooms does.

When permits are required, they must be obtained before any work regulated under the permit is started. The permits are normally required to be posted at the job site, in a conspicuous place, where they can be easily seen. Failure to comply with code regulations can result in fines, and (sometimes) imprisonment.

Getting a Permit

Getting permit isn't difficult, but there are guidelines that must be followed. The procedure for obtaining a permit can vary from jurisdiction to jurisdiction. Check with your local code authorities for exact details about requirements.

Typically, a set of plans and specifications must be submitted to the code-enforcement office, along with a completed permit application (available from the code office) before you receive a permit.

Some types of work may not require submission of plans and specifications. In such cases, the only paperwork involved will be the permit application. There will be a fee for the permit, if it's issued. The fees vary from location to location, but the costs for all the permits needed for a major remodeling job can run into hundreds of dollars. Permits are usually issued only to homeowners who will be performing the work themselves, and to licensed contractors. If you apply for the permit in your name and then hire an unlicensed contractor to do the work, there could be trouble if you're caught.

Once you've applied for the permit, a code officer will review the application. If all the paperwork is in order, the permit fee will be paid (by you or by your contractor) and the permit will be issued. The permit should be posted at your home in a way that an inspector can see it from the street.

Which Types of Work Require Permits?

Most small jobs that are mostly repairs or maintenance don't normally require permits and inspections, but larger jobs do. Permits are likely to be needed for the work described below.

Plumbing

Plumbing almost always requires a permit and inspection. Unless all you'll be doing is very minor remodeling or repair work, plan on getting a plumbing permit. If you'll be replacing fixtures, adding fixtures, or doing extensive work with plumbing pipes, a permit and inspections will usually be required.

Electrical

If you'll be adding circuits, relocating wiring, or doing any work of such nature, a permit will probably be required.

HVAC

Heating and air-conditioning work also usually requires a permit. Very minor changes won't require a permit or inspection, but if you expand your HVAC system or make sig-

nificant changes in outlet locations, you may need a permit.

Building

Building permits are usually required whenever a new structure is built, but they may not be required for cosmetic remodeling. Structural changes to your home may likely require a permit.

Inquire at your local code-enforcement office for information on what's required of you. Code requirements can change quickly, and each jurisdiction can have its own set of rules.

Keep Your Contractors Honest

If a permit and/or an inspection is required, insist that your contractors comply with the regulations. While it may not be your responsibility to see that contractors obtain the proper permits, you may be the one eventually to suffer if they don't.

A contractor's serious violation of code requirements could jeopardize your health and safety. For example, there are many plumbing-code requirements that exist for your protection. If an air gap is not installed with the drainage system of a dishwasher, it's possible that contaminated water in the drainage pipes will flow back into the dishwasher, creating a health hazard. If a plumber omits a required vent pipe, you may suffer from the effects of sewer gas. Water heaters that are installed without relief valves could explode!

An electrician's failure to install a ground-fault interceptor could result in a fatal shock. Aside from the more deadly infractions, minor code violations can make your job less functional. If electrical outlets are not installed at the prescribed minimum distances, an appliance's electrical cord may be too short to reach an outlet.

If a heating technician installs heating units in the wrong locations, the performance of the heating system may not be satisfactory.

In addition to the health risks and inconvenience you might encounter with work done in a nonconforming manner, you might lose a substantial amount of money because of the violations. If an electrician gave you a great price for rewiring your kitchen and did the job without a permit, what might happen? The house could burn down. You could be electrocuted. An electrical inspector from the code-enforcement office might require all the kitchen walls to be torn open so wiring could be inspected if an illegal job is discovered.

If you're forced to destroy your new job for the sake of an inspection that was never done, who'll pay for the damage? It seems the offending contractor should, but suppose the contractor has gone out of business or left town, what then? You may be left holding the responsibility. All of your work must be done in compliance with code requirements.

12
Financing

What's involved in financing your remodeling? Can you just walk into your bank and ask for a loan and get it? Should you take out a personal loan to pay for the job, or should you refinance your house to cover the costs?

Major remodeling jobs are often quite expensive, forcing many people to seek loans. The task of finding and selecting the best loan can be arduous. There are many forms of financing to consider.

Does the Type of Financing You Choose Really Make a Difference?

The type of financing you choose can make a big difference in the long-term cost of your job. The interest you pay on the loan will increase the overall cost of remodeling. If you have to pay a lender financing points to originate the loan, you'll need more money to start the job.

Your choice of a loan can also affect how much income tax you'll pay. If you use the loan as part of your home mortgage, the interest on the loan may be deductible, resulting in less taxes due.

If you're thinking of selling your home, the financing you choose could hamper the sale. Your house may have an assumable mortgage, with an attractive interest rate. Selling the house with the assumable loan may give you a great advantage in a real-estate market with high interest rates. However, if you refinance the house at higher interest rates to pay for a new kitchen, you may lose your sales advantage.

Selecting a loan is a responsibility that shouldn't be taken lightly. Knowing how to apply for a loan can lead to having the loan approved.

Fixed-Rate Loans

Most people are best informed about fixed-rate loans. You borrow money at an agreed-upon interest rate, and the rate never changes. The biggest advantage to this type of loan is that you know what your payments will be for each installment over the life of the loan. The biggest disadvantage to a fixed-rate loan is that the rate is usually higher when the loan is obtained than are the rates for other types of loans.

If you plan to keep your house for at least ten years, and you're not much of a gambler, fixed-rate loans will probably suit you best. People who want to save money on the first few years of their loan and who aren't afraid of a little risk will usually do better with an adjustable-rate loan.

Adjustable-Rate Loans

Adjustable-rate loans are common, and they offer many advantages. Interest rates for adjustable-rate loans can (and usually do) fluctuate. The rates typically go up, rather than down, but they can go down. There are many variations of adjustable-rate loans; some are better than others.

Most adjustable-rate loans are adjusted annually, but others may be adjusted semi-annually, or at other intervals. These loans are tied to specific indexes that affect how they are adjusted: treasury bills are one of the common indexes.

Since lenders don't make long-term commitments for interest rates on adjustable loans, the starting interest rates are often very attractive. Many adjustable-rate loans have starting interest rates several points lower than fixed-rate loans. This can save you money in the early years of the loan.

Adjustable-rate loans that have annual and lifetime *caps* are safer than loans without caps. Caps limit the amount of increase allowed in the interest rate of the loan. For example, if a loan has an annual cap of 2%, the interest rate can not go up or down more than 2% in any given year. When the loan has a lifetime cap of 6%, the loan can never go up or down by more than 6%. For instance, if the loan has an initial interest rate of 8%, and the lifetime cap of the loan is 6%, the interest rate could never go above 14%. Loans without caps should be avoided; there are no limits on how high the rates can rise for these loans.

There are so many types of adjustable-rate loans available that each loan must be studied carefully. Avoid loans that don't have annual and lifetime caps, and those that allow *negative amortization*. With negative amortization your payments can be very low, but after paying on the loan for five years you may owe more than you borrowed. Negative amortization allows interest that is not being paid (to keep the payments low) to accrue, resulting in a higher loan balance than the one you started with.

If you plan to sell your house within five years of completing your remodeling project, an adjustable-rate loan could be a real money-saver.

In-Home Financing

Many contractors offer *in-home* financing plans. These plans are easy to apply for and are almost always approved if the applicant has equity in his home. There are many types of in-home financing plans. These plans typically charge a much higher interest rate than what a credit union or commercial bank would. However, points and closing costs are rarely an expensive factor with in-home financing.

An in-home financing contract is similar, in many ways, to the financing offered by car dealers. There are times when this type of financing is worth considering, but normally you can do better by dealing with your bank or credit union.

Finance Companies

Finance companies like to make second mortgages to homeowners who have plenty of equity in their homes. The rates and terms offered by financing companies fluctuate, but they are rarely as good as those available from credit unions and banks.

Ask Your Lawyer

Before you sign any financing agreement, consult your lawyer. When you give a lender a mortgage against your home, the wrong words in the financing agreement could cause you to lose your house. While most banks use standard financing agreements, not all notes and mortgages are the same. When you deal with private financing from finance companies and in-home financing plans, you may encounter some strange and undesirable language in the financing terms and agreement.

Financing Fees

Financing fees can add to the cost of your job. You know that the interest you pay on a loan over the coming years will increase the investment made in remodeling, but you may not be aware of some of the more immediate costs.

Loan Application Fees

Most lenders require you to pay a loan application fee, which is usually nonrefundable and can vary in cost.

Credit-Reporting Fees

Credit-reporting fees, usually required at the time of loan application, are rarely refundable, and their costs also vary.

Appraisal

When you apply for a large loan, the lender will usually require an appraisal of your property. The rules for when an appraisal is required vary from lender to lender, but if you plan a complete bath or kitchen remodeling job, plan on the cost of an appraisal. Appraisal fees vary from location to location, and lender to lender, but budget at least several hundred dollars for the fee, and don't be surprised if it costs more. Call your intended lender to determine the exact cost.

Points

"Points" are fees equal to 1% of the loan amount. In other words, if the loan amount is $20,000, a fee of two "points" will be $400. These points are sometimes called origination fees, discount points, or prepaid interest.

Title Searches

Title searches, usually required when a house is being used as security for a loan, reveal any outstanding liens or encumbrances that affect a homeowner's equity position. Fees for title searches vary.

Surveys

If your kitchen or bathroom remodeling calls for adding space onto your home, expect to pay for a survey. A lender will want to be sure your addition is on your property and is in compliance with zoning regulations. Survey costs can vary greatly, depending on the size of your lot and the type of survey required by the lender.

Other Closing Costs

Other closing costs that will have to be paid when you borrow money for remodeling might include legal fees, filing fees, and other types of fees. Any reputable lender will provide you with an estimate of what your closing costs will be before you sign a loan.

How Much Will a Loan Add to the Cost of Your Job?

It will depend on where you borrow the money and what the individual lender charges, as well as what the interest rates are.

Assume you'll be doing a major kitchen remodeling, and that the amount of money borrowed from your bank will be $20,000. The interest rate is 10%, and the loan is a fixed-rate with a 15-year term. You'll make monthly payments of about $215 for 180 months. The total amount of these payments will be $38,700, nearly twice what you originally paid for the job. Such figures can be real eye-openers.

With money borrowed from an "in-home" financing plan, the interest rate is 11.5%, and the rest of the terms are the same. Payments for this loan will be about $234 a month. This doesn't sound like a big difference, but the total cost, using this financing, will be $42,120, or $3,420 more than using bank financing.

Loan Applications

Once you decide to finance your job, prepare to make a loan application. Although this isn't a complicated process, it helps to have all your documents in order. There may be many items a lender wants before he approves your loan.

Getting a personal loan differs from getting a loan based on the value of the home improvements. You'll need less documentation for a personal loan. Let's look at your needs for a successful loan application, as we examine them on the assumption that the home improvements will be a factor in the loan approval. If you have plenty of equity in your home or if you have a strong line of credit, you won't need all of the items discussed below.

Plans & Specifications

If a loan is being based on the value of an intended home improvement, the lender will want plans and specifications. The lender will review your plans and specs and will probably have a before-and-after appraisal done on your home.

Permits

Some lenders require all necessary permits be purchased before granting a home improvement loan. This assures the lender that the work will be done with the necessary code approvals.

Tax Returns

Some lenders want to see tax returns for the last two years. This usually isn't required, unless you're self-employed.

Bank Accounts

You'll be asked to list all of your bank accounts. Account numbers will be needed, and you must identify the type of accounts you have (such as checkings and savings).

Financial Statements

While you won't need a formal financial statement (unless you're self-employed),

you will have to list all of your assets and liabilities. The liabilities will include credit-card debt, car loans, school loans, and any other financial obligations you have. Account numbers will be needed for each loan you have outstanding.

Social Security Number

Your social security number is required on loan applications. If you don't know what yours is, find out, and bring it along with you to the loan-application office.

Employment History

If you have had different jobs in the last five years, be prepared to list the dates of your employment, the locations, your earnings, your supervisor, and the buyer's address.

Previous Addresses

Be prepared to provide detailed information about your previous addresses.

Credit References

There will be space on the loan application for listing credit references. Be prepared to provide account numbers and addresses for the references.

Other Information

If you've been divorced, you may be required to provide a copy of the divorce decree. If you have had credit problems in the past, be prepared to explain, in writing, why you had trouble maintaining good credit.

Once the Formal Application Is Made

Once the formal loan application is made, all you can do is wait. The process can be as short as a week or as long as two months. You will normally be notified by mail whether your loan is approved or denied.

If the loan is approved, a closing date will be arranged. This will be the day you sign all the papers and receive the money to begin your project. Loan closings are usually simple procedures that take less than an hour to complete. You may wish to take your attorney to the closing with you, since the papers you sign may affect your position of ownership in your home.

All the preliminary work is now out of the way, so let's get involved with the remodeling work itself.

13
Demolition

Demolition involved with remodeling a kitchen or bathroom can be a major undertaking, depending upon existing conditions and the degree of demolition needed. The job could consume days of your time. Demolition can also be dangerous to you and your house. If you don't follow proper procedures, you could, for example, electrocute yourself, or flood your home.

Should you do your own demolition? If you're in good health and you're handy, you shouldn't have any trouble doing your own demolition. However, you should have an understanding of what's involved in the process before you begin.

There are some safety hazards involved with demolition. Eye protection should be worn at all times, and hearing protection may be needed for some parts of the job. Proper clothing and footwear can protect you from cuts, scratches, and punctures. Some demolition work may be done while you stand on a ladder, so exercise caution to avoid falling.

It's important that you know that there are dangers involved in remodeling, which are present throughout the job. If you don't know how to work safely with tools, ladders, and general remodeling, consult books about safety.

Preparation

Preparing for demolition work in advance, you'll be able to avoid many problems. One of the first problems that the inexperienced encounter in demolition is the mess that it makes in the rest of the home. There's much dust and debris involved with demolition, and keeping the mess contained in the room being ripped out is the first order of business.

Disposing of Debris

Before you can begin the containment process, you must have a plan for disposing of the debris. If the room being remodeled has a window or door that opens to the outside, you may be able to place a trash container near the opening and toss the debris out as you go along. This not only controls clutter in the workplace, it also makes the job go faster. If you have to pile the rubbish in the room and then haul it out to a trash container, you handle the materials twice.

If you work in a second- or third-floor room, build a chute for your trash removal. Set a trash container below the upstairs window from which you'll be discarding debris. Use framing lumber and plywood to build a trash chute. The chute should have side rails that prevent debris from falling over the sides. The chute will resemble a sliding board. Have the chute extend from the trash container to the window, and secure it firmly.

Dust Containment

If you don't seal off the room you're remodeling from the rest of your home, dust will settle everywhere. The work involved in dust containment is very easy. All you need is some plastic and some duct tape.

Seal all doors and other openings between the workspace and the rest of the home with sheets of plastic. Cut the sheets larger than the openings you are covering, and allow the plastic to extend several inches past the frame of the opening. Use duct tape to attach the plastic to the walls of the room you're working in. Keep the plastic on the side of the opening where you will be working, not on the side of the rest of your home. Tape the plastic to the walls and floor using long strips of tape. Don't leave any portion of the seams untaped.

If, for access to the room being remodeled, you must use a door that opens into other living space, you may want to use an alternative method for sealing the opening. Pulling tape loose from the walls and floor each time you want to enter or exit a room can be annoying.

Cut an extra-large sheet of plastic to cover an entrance. Tape the top and one side of the plastic to the walls (as described above). Attach a 2×4 to the bottom of the plastic and roll the plastic around the piece of wood until the vertical fit of the plastic is tight. The weight of the wood will hold the plastic down, and you won't have to tape the plastic to the floor.

On the remaining side of the opening, tape the plastic to the wall at the top, middle, and bottom, but don't use long strips of tape; small pieces will do fine. There will be gaps along this edge of the plastic. Left alone, these gaps will allow dust to escape the room. To remedy this situation without sealing yourself in tightly, hang a second piece of plastic to overlap the lightly taped edge.

The second sheet of plastic should be taped to the wall at the top and along one edge with long strips of tape. The section of plastic that overlaps the other plastic should be taped at the top, middle, and bottom with the use of a minimal amount of tape. When this is done, the room is sealed, but you can come and go easily. All you

have to do to open the exit is to pull the tape from the bottom and middle section of the overlap and the inner plastic. The bottom of the main covering will move easily when you push the wood to one side. This arrangement controls dust while allowing reasonable ingress and egress.

Demolishing a Bathroom

If you'll be stripping a room down to bare studs and subfloor, there will be much work involved. You'll be working with plumbing and electrical devices, and you may have to work with part of your heating system. These mechanical systems must be treated with respect. The job may also involve removing wall coverings, ceilings, and floor coverings. While most homeowners have little problem demolishing a bathroom, there are some things to be careful of.

Assume that you have your bathroom prepared for demolition and that you're equipped with the proper safety devices. In this hypothetical job, none of the existing fixtures will be salvaged. The logical place to begin is with the plumbing fixtures.

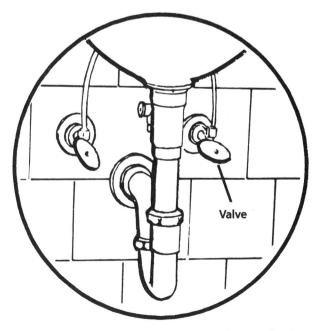

Illus. 13-1. Valve location for a bathroom basin. Drawing courtesy of USDA Forest Service

Plumbing

Before you begin tearing out old plumbing, make sure the water supply to the fixtures is turned off. Don't assume a closed valve (Illus. 13-1) has stopped the water; some valves fail with age. After you close the appropriate valves, test each fixture to see that the water is, in fact, shut off.

Begin by removing the toilet. A screwdriver and an adjustable wrench are the only tools you should need. Flush the toilet to evacuate most of the water. Remove the nuts on the bolts extending through the base of the toilet. If the nuts won't turn, they can be cut off with a hacksaw blade. Loosen the nut that secures the water supply to the toilet tank. The toilet can now be lifted off the floor and removed.

A complete toilet can be awkward and heavy to handle for the inexperienced. In most cases, the tank of the toilet can be separated from the bowl, making removal easy. Removable toilet tanks are attached with brass bolts and nuts. By putting a screwdriver in the head of the bolt and turning the nuts, the tank should be easy to remove. Sometimes the bolts are stubborn and you'll need a hacksaw blade to cut them. If you decide to break the toilet into pieces with a hammer, be aware that broken china can inflict nasty wounds.

With the toilet out of the way, move on to the lavatory. Disconnect the trap from the fixture; this can usually be done with a set of wide-jaw pliers. The water supplies must also be disconnected. You should be able to easily loosen the small compression nuts that hold the supply tubes into the cutoff valves. Once the waste and water lines are loose, remove the basin.

If you have a wall-hung lavatory, it should lift straight up and off its wall bracket. Some wall-hung lavatories are secured to the wall with lag bolts. If you can't lift the bowl off the bracket, look for bolts securing it to the wall. If you can't find any, exert some extra pressure to remove the lavatory.

If your bathroom has a vanity and a top, the removal process is different. The vanity top is probably attached to the wall with caulking. Run a knife along the joints where the top meets the wall. Look to see if the top is attached to the vanity or simply resting atop it. Remove any screws holding the top to the cabinet and the top should lift off. Before trying to remove the base cabinet, check to see if it's screwed to the wall.

With the lavatory and toilet out of the way, you'll have more space to remove the bathtub. Before you remove the tub, remove the walls that overlap its edges. Strip the walls surrounding the bathtub to reveal the tub edges.

A hammer works well to remove the walls. Don't cut into the walls blindly with a saw: you might hit live electrical wires. Beat holes in the walls with a hammer and pull the wall covering off. If you must use a saw, open the walls with a hammer and check for wiring and plumbing before sawing.

When you have the walls around the tub stripped to the bare studs, you can start removing the tub. Remove the tub faucet first, but be sure that the water to the pipes is turned off. Unlike the other fixtures, the faucet for the bathtub won't have small supply tubes; it will be connected directly to $\frac{1}{2}''$ tubing or pipe. There may be unions in the pipes to make removal easy, but you will probably have to cut the pipes with a hacksaw blade or with pipe cutters.

The next step is to remove the tub waste and overflow. From inside the bathtub, remove the screws holding the trim on the overflow. If the drain has a strainer on it, remove the screw securing the strainer and expose the cross-bars in the drain. Using two thick-shaft screwdrivers, insert the screwdrivers into the drain and cross the shafts. By creating an "X" with the screwdrivers, you'll be able to loosen and remove the drain. Turn the drain counterclockwise to unscrew it.

When all the plumbing connections are loose, remove the tub. If the bathtub is a one-piece tub-shower combination, it should be secured to the stud walls by nails or screws. Once the tub is free of the walls, you'll probably have to cut it into sections. One-piece tub-shower units won't usually fit through interior doors or travel up or down finished stairs. You can cut the unit into pieces using a hacksaw blade, but the job will go more quickly when you use a reciprocating saw.

Standard bathtubs (ones without shower walls) are not normally attached to the stud walls; they rest on supports. To remove a standard tub, lift and slide it out of the opening. This sounds easier than it sometimes is.

Plastic, fiberglass, and steel bathtubs can be removed without too much strain, but cast-iron tubs are another matter entirely. Cast-iron tubs can weigh over 400 pounds and wrestling one out of its resting place can be very difficult, even for seasoned professionals. Many professionals use sledgehammers to break cast-iron tubs into manageable pieces. If you do this, wear eye and ear protection, along with clothing that will protect you from flying sharp pieces of tub.

Heating

You may not have to do much with the heating system in your bathroom. If your heat comes in through ducts in the floor, just remove the register from the duct and protect the open duct from falling debris. You can stuff a towel in the duct or cut a piece of plywood to cover the opening.

If you have hot-water baseboard heat, remove the baseboard heating element. This will require shutting down the boiler, and it may require draining the heating system. If you're working on the top floor of your home, you shouldn't need to drain much water from the heating system before cut-

ting the supply and return pipes at the baseboard unit. However, if there is heat installed in rooms above your bathroom, drain the heating system to a point below the bathroom.

There will be removable end-caps on the baseboard heating unit. Remove these caps by pulling them off to reveal the supply and return pipes. The pipes should be copper, and they can be cut using a hacksaw or a pipe cutter. Once the pipes are cut, remove the screws that hold the baseboard unit to the wall and remove the heating unit.

If you have an old house that's equipped with radiators, try to avoid removing them. Old radiators can become damaged when moved, and they are difficult and expensive to replace.

Electrical

Now that all the plumbing and heating is out of the way, you'll be ready to work with electrical devices and fixtures. Turn off the power to the bathroom. Use an electrical meter to test each wire before working with it. If you don't know how to use an electrical meter, don't work with electricity; call in a professional.

With the power turned off, remove all cover plates from switches and outlets. Remove the globes or shades on your lights, and remove the light bulbs. Most electrical fixtures are attached to their electrical boxes with a threaded rod and nuts. Remove these nuts and the fixture should come loose. Remove the wire nuts (plastic covers protecting the wires) and test for electricity.

When you're sure the power is off, separate the fixture wires from the house wiring. Install wire nuts on the house wiring and tuck it back into the electrical box.

If you have electric baseboard heat, it should be attached to the wall by screws. Before handling the wiring to the heat, make sure the electricity is off. Don't count on all of your bathroom wiring being on the same circuit. Just because a bulb doesn't light up doesn't mean that the heat is safe to work with.

Walls & Ceilings

Removing finished walls and ceilings made of drywall isn't difficult. Use a hammer to open the walls and ceiling and to expose all wiring, plumbing, and heating. Use a dust mask to protect you from the massive amounts of dust this process creates. Then, either continue to demolish the walls and ceiling with a hammer, or you can cut out the drywall using a saw. Window and door trim will also have to be removed during this stage.

If you have plaster walls, you'll have much more work to do. A reciprocating saw is the fastest way to cut through plaster and the lath behind it. Use a hammer to open sections of the wall before running the saw through the plaster, since it's easy to cut wires and plumbing by accident.

Flooring

Removing vinyl flooring isn't difficult. Start by removing all baseboard trim and shoe molding. When the molding is removed, the edges of the flooring will be exposed. You may be able to grasp the ends and pull up the flooring. If the flooring is difficult to remove, use a floor scraper to remove it.

If you'll be removing a ceramic-tile floor, chisel the tiles up or smash them with a hammer. Remember to protect your eyes and body from sharp slivers.

Odds & Ends

Go around the bathroom and remove all nails that protrude from the walls and ceiling. Sweep the floor and scrape it until it's clean. Cap all pipes to keep debris from entering them. Make sure all electrical wires are protected with wire nuts. Look around and tidy up any loose ends.

The principles used to rip out a bathroom also apply to kitchens, although the material you'll work with will differ.

14
The Unexpected

You'll probably encounter some unexpected conditions when you begin to remodel. You can plan to achieve a perfect job, but you can't always plan for the unexpected. If you know in advance which types of conditions may exist, you'll be prepared.

Professionals sometimes have problems created by existing conditions. The water pipes, at some time, may have frozen and then swollen to a point where fittings won't slide over them. The problem could be a wall that isn't plumb or a floor that isn't level. When you install kitchen cabinets, it's very important to have level floors and plumb walls.

While most unexpected problems have to

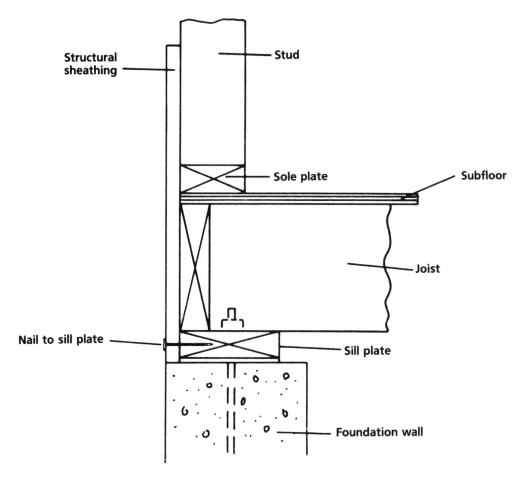

Illus. 14-1. Detail of an exterior wall, showing floor joists. Drawing courtesy of USDA Forest Service

95

do with building materials and conditions, it isn't unusual to encounter other types of problems. When you open an existing wall you never know what you might find. There could be a nest of bees hiding behind the drywall or an angry rodent. If you remove the ceiling in a kitchen that has its own attic, you may be surprised to see a swarm of startled bats. Crawling under the house to work on the plumbing might bring you face to face with a snake or feral cat.

I have encountered skunks, rattlesnakes, rats, squirrels, feral cats, bats, bees, porcupines, and other types of wildlife during my remodeling career. Most of the encounters ended amicably, but some were frightening. If you're aware of what you might find, you'll be prepared to deal with the problems.

Where?

Floors

When you work with your floors, you may find that the subfloor (Illus. 14-1) or the floor joists must be replaced. The damaged floor may not be evident until you remove the finish floor covering. Water damage is a frequent cause for this type of problem, but the problem could result from termites or other wood-infesting insects. The floor joists may simply have rotted to a point where they're no longer structurally sound.

Walls & Ceilings

Walls and ceilings can conceal many potential problems. When cavities behind finished walls and ceilings (Illus. 14-2) are exposed, you may find that the insulation has become dilapidated, or you may even find that insulation was never installed. This can engender unexpected labor and material.

Bees and snakes often take up residence in hollow walls. It can be very unnerving to cut out a wall section and be swarmed by angry bees, or to see a big snake slither out of sight in the wall.

The wall studs could be covered with the telltale sign of termites. You'll have to replace the damaged studs, and you'll need expensive professional termite extermination.

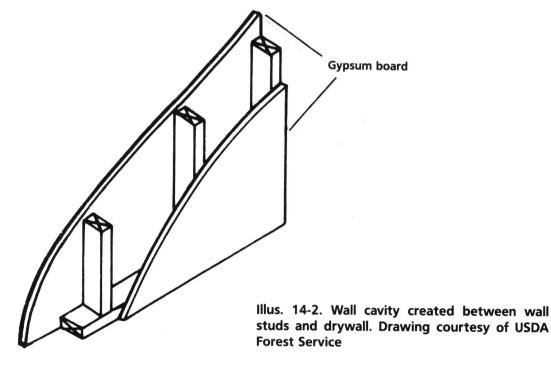

Gypsum board

Illus. 14-2. Wall cavity created between wall studs and drywall. Drawing courtesy of USDA Forest Service

The bottom plate of your wall may have rotted, causing much more extensive work to the wall than you expected.

Removing a ceiling can reveal water damage to the floor above you. There are many times when leaking plumbing fixtures and water damage go undetected until a ceiling is removed.

Most attics have insulation between the ceiling joists, on the back side of the ceiling you are working with. Cutting out a section of this type of ceiling and getting a face full of loose insulation is unpleasant.

Attics can also be home to bats, birds, snakes, rats, mice, squirrels, and even raccoons. If the ceiling you'll be working with has an attic above it, inspect it before opening the ceiling.

Mechanical Systems

Mechanical systems can cause much frustration. You may think you are working with copper plumbing pipes only to discover that they're brass. Old brass pipe can be cut with standard copper cutters, but copper fittings won't usually slide over brass pipe. You might find that the electrical wiring in your kitchen was run in a haphazard way, and that some wires are dead while others are hot. This can be a *shocking* experience.

Most mechanical problems can be overcome with minimal trouble, but some may be serious. For example, you may discover that your toilet wasn't mounted to a flange, and that the pipe connecting to the toilet was an old-fashioned lead bend. If this is the case, your main drainage system is old enough to be made of cast-iron pipe, and converting it to plastic pipe will require a special soil-pipe cutter.

If you relocate a radiator that provides heat to your room, you may find that it leaks when you reinstall it. This can be expensive and frustrating to correct.

Cabinets

Installing cabinets is very difficult if you don't have level floors and plumb walls to work with. You may spend many hours installing shims to get the cabinets to fit properly. If you don't take the time to level the cabinets, the doors and drawers won't work smoothly.

Countertops

When you install your new countertop, you may discover that your walls are very much out of plumb, resulting in the top being tight against the wall at one point, with a gap at another point. If you don't know that the wall is out of plumb until you install the countertop, the cost of your job will escalate. If the gap is significant, you'll have to remove the finished wall covering and use furring strips to build the wall out, or order a new countertop. Either way, you'll lose time and money. Check the walls early on in your job.

Appliances

It's embarrassing to have a freshly remodeled kitchen and new appliances that won't fit in the openings you provided for them. A mere ¼″ can prevent you from sliding a new refrigerator into its opening, so verify the dimensions of all appliances and fixtures before you create space for them.

Under the House

If work entails having to crawl under your house, you may find unexpected problems. Your floor joists could be riddled with holes from powder-post beetles. Water could be standing under the home, creating mold and rotting your wood. There's always the chance that animals will be seeking shelter in your crawl space, so don't go under the house without proper lighting. While you're under your home, look for any defects that might exist; fix them before the problem escalates.

Looking Ahead

Looking ahead is the best way to avoid serious problems. If you consider what could be on the inside of a wall or under a floor, you'll be less likely to experience trouble with your remodeling. For example, failure to think about wires that are installed in a wall could cause you to cut them with a saw, perhaps resulting in electrical shock, and it will certainly result in additional work. Think before you act.

15
Putting It Back Together

After you've successfully completed the demolition, it will be time to put it all back together. You may need some help from friends or contractors, but the job is manageable.

Restoring your kitchen or bath will go smoothly if you do it in an organized manner. There will be much work to do, and some of the work will be far more difficult if it isn't done with the proper timing. For example, should you install your countertop before or after you paint your walls? Most contractors paint first and then install countertops.

Why do they do it in this order? If the counter is installed first, there will be no paint on the wall behind the counter. This means the painter will have to paint right up to the edge of the counter, without getting paint on it. Painting the room will be much more difficult with the cabinets and countertops already installed. Access to the walls won't be as good, and there's always the risk of spilling paint on expensive cabinets and counters.

Some believe that countertops should be installed before a room is painted, because freshly painted walls may be scuffed when the counters are installed. It's probable that some scuffing will occur, but it's much easier to touch up a few nicks with the counter in place than it is to paint all the walls with the counter in the way. Proper planning and scheduling can make your job run more smoothly.

Production Schedule

Before you begin your work, create a production schedule. Organize all the work that will need to be done into a logical sequence. Break the work down into phases, such as rough-in plumbing and final plumbing. It's unlikely that your schedule will work out the way you design it, but by having a written production schedule, you'll be less likely to overlook work that needs to be done, and you'll have a better chance of keeping the job on track.

Once you have a list of all the types of work required in your job, assign dates to each task. For example, schedule rough plumbing for June 10th and rough electrical work for June 11th. Remember to allow time for code inspections. Some phases of your job won't be able to progress until other phases are inspected and approved. For example, you can't hang drywall and conceal rough plumbing and electrical work until these are inspected and approved.

When you have tentative dates for all the various work phases, note the work that contractors will be doing for you. This will enable you to give contractors plenty of notice before their services will be required. If part of the job doesn't go according to schedule, remember to change the dates for all aspects of the work that will be affected.

It is unlikely that you'll know how much time to allow for the various types of work.

If you'll be doing all the work yourself, the exact timing won't be as critical as it might if you use contractors. However, even if you do the work yourself, develop a rough idea of when various phases will be complete. Otherwise, you won't be able to project the dates for ordering cabinets, countertops, and other supplies.

It may take several attempts before you have your production schedule revised until it's reasonably accurate. If you'll be using contractors, ask them to provide estimates for the amount of time they'll need to complete their work.

Schedule Production in Logical Order

Not being an experienced general contractor, or remodeler, you'll be unlikely to know what a logical order is. All time es-timates are based on work done by professionals, so adjust the amount of time to compensate for your own skill levels.

Preparation

Preparation is the first phase of any remodeling job. Make arrangements for trash removal and dust control. Permits must often be obtained at this stage. Preparation can usually be completed in one day.

Demolition

Demolition is the next step. Before you begin tearing out what's there, order the materials needed for reconstruction. Check with your suppliers to determine how much advance notice he'll require to have various items delivered when you want them. For example, you can probably get a load of

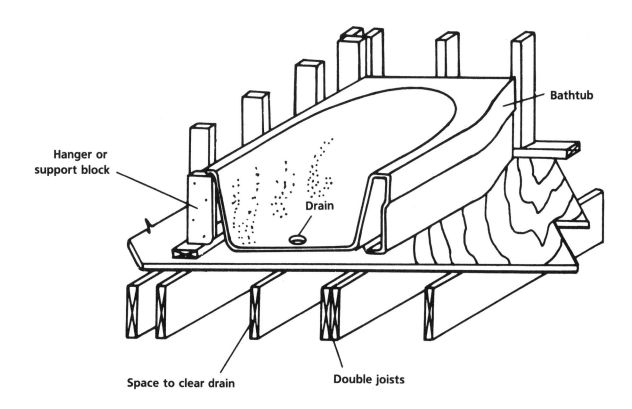

Illus. 15-1. Cutaway view of a bathtub in its rough framing. Drawing courtesy of USDA Forest Service

lumber in a day or two, but it could take weeks to get new cabinets.

Demolishing a bathroom can often be done in one day, but it could take two or three days to strip down kitchens to the bare studs and subfloor.

Rough Framing

If you are relocating or adding walls, do it now. Framing work often requires a building permit and an inspection. If you plan to install underlayment on your subfloor, do it in the rough-framing phase. Most framing for interior bathroom (Illus. 15-1) and kitchen remodeling can be completed in a day or two.

Rough Plumbing

Once the demolition is done, make any plumbing adjustments needed in the rough plumbing. If you'll be installing a new bathtub or shower, this is the time to do it. This work usually requires a permit and inspection. The rough plumbing for a kitchen or bathroom rarely takes more than a day to complete.

Heating

Heating work is normally done after the plumbing is done and before the electrical work begins. You may need a permit and

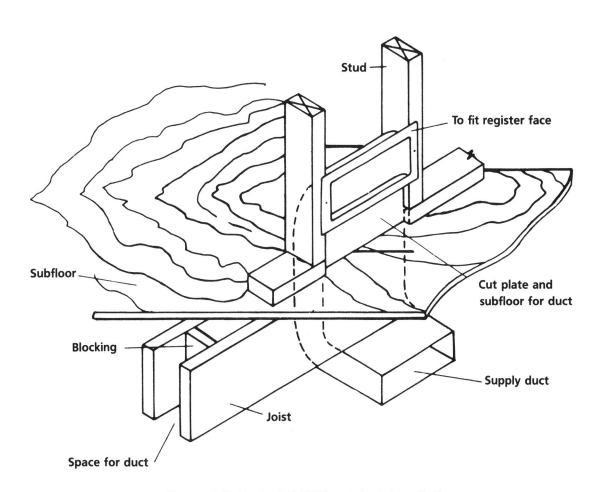

**Illus. 15-2. Typical HVAC heat-duct installation.
Drawing courtesy of USDA Forest Service**

inspection for the heating work required in your job. The heating work required for a typical kitchen or bath remodeling job (Illus. 15-2) should take no more than one day.

Electrical

Electrical work typically follows plumbing and heating. Again, a permit and inspection may be required. This work should be completed in one day.

Insulation

If you have to insulate, do it after the plumbing, heating, and electrical work has been done and inspected. Many code jurisdictions require insulation to be inspected prior to concealment. The building permit you obtained should include insulation work. Installing insulation doesn't take long, but allow one day for it.

Drywall

Once all the mechanical work and insulation is installed and inspected, you'll be ready for drywall. This work is included in the building permit, but it often requires an inspection.

After the drywall is hung and taped, it has to be finished. During this lengthy process, you'll be unable to do much of anything else. Three coats of joint compound are typically installed on new drywall seams, corners, and dimples. Each coat of compound must dry and be sanded before the next layer is applied. Sanding is very dusty work.

Drywall can be hung on the walls and ceiling of a room in a day. The taping and first coat of compound can also be installed on the first day. By the second day, the second coat of compound can usually be applied, and by the beginning of the fourth day the walls and ceilings should be ready to paint.

Painting

Generally at least one coat of primer and one coat of paint is used, and this work will take at least two days.

Finish Flooring

Finish flooring is usually done next. This part of the job doesn't require a special inspection, and it should be completed in one day.

Cabinets, Counters & Fixtures

The cabinets, counters, and fixtures can be installed after the finish flooring is laid. Individual inspections aren't required for this work. These items will be inspected during final inspections.

A good kitchen remodeling crew can hang and set all the cabinets in a standard kitchen in one day, but allow them at least two days for the job. Professional plumbers can set all the fixtures for a bathroom or kitchen in less than one day. Electricians and heating mechanics (when setting fixtures) can be in and out in one day.

Trim

Once all the cabinets and fixtures are in, the trim work can be done. Some people install trim before fixtures and cabinets are installed, but others do it afterwards. Either way will work, but I prefer to have the trim installed afterwards: it always seems to fit better that way.

Most professionals paint or stain the trim before they install it. All that will be required once the trim is in place is to fill nail holes and to touch up the paint or stain. Installing trim can be time-consuming, but any good professional can trim a kitchen or bath in one day.

Final Touches

There may be many small final touches before the job can be considered finished. These odds and ends can take a day or two to complete.

Cleaning Up

Cleaning up the mess and cleaning the new fixtures should take less than one day.

Final Inspections

Once the job is completely finished, you'll be ready for final inspections. This may involve a visit from a plumbing inspector, an electrical inspector, an HVAC inspector, and a building inspector.

Some jobs will require work not mentioned in this outline, such as tile work or decorative stenciling. The list of work described above should give you a good idea of how to plan your production schedule. There's little doubt you'll have to make adjustments, but with some advance planning and effort, you can make your job run more smoothly by using a production schedule.

16
Flooring

The right floor coverings can distinguish the room and make a statement about its owner. The wrong floor covering can darken the room or give an unbalanced appearance. You choice of floor covering will have a strong effect on the overall appearance of your remodeled room. See the color photos on pages 68, 69, 70, 125, and 128.

Even with the best available floor covering, bad subflooring and floor joists can prevent your room from being outstanding. If the floor squeaks every time you walk across it, you'll notice the squeak more than you will the attractive floor covering. If the joists are weak and the floor is spongy, you may wonder when your refrigerator is going to fall through the floor.

Most of the work done in routine kitchen and bathroom remodeling isn't structural, but the flooring is. While you don't need superior framing skills to build a linen closet, you may need them to repair damaged floor joists. It's uncommon to discover rotted or damaged floor joists, but it does happen. What would you do if you removed water-stained subflooring and you found that the tops of three floor joists had rotted badly? Many would panic and assume the joist would have to be removed and replaced. It's possible that the joists would need replacement, but it's more likely that a minor repair could solve the problem.

In this chapter you'll learn about floor joists, subflooring, underlayment, and finished floor coverings. There will be tips on how to handle rotten joists the easy way,

and how to get the bubbles out of your new vinyl flooring.

Floor Joists

Floor joists (Illustrations 16-1, 16-2) are the structural members that support the subfloor. They're usually boards with dimensions ranging from 2×8 to 2×12. Floor joists span the distances between outside walls and support girders. The length of the span and the use of the floor influence the size of the joist.

If you remove your subfloor and find a few of the floor joists to be rotted, you may not have to replace them. It's possible that you could add new supports without removing the old ones. In many cases all you'll have to do is to slide new joists in place on each side of the damaged joist and nail them to the old joist. The new joists should be of the same length and have the same dimensions as the old joist. This usually isn't a very difficult procedure, and it will work well in most circumstances.

If only a small section of a joist is damaged, you may be able to get by with "scabbing" new pieces of wood onto the old joist. Assume an existing joist is damaged, but only for about two feet of its length. You could attach new wood on each side of the damaged area to avoid installing complete joists. The "scab" wood should extend well past the damaged area; in this case, scab wood about four feet long should be sufficient. This practice may not be suitable in

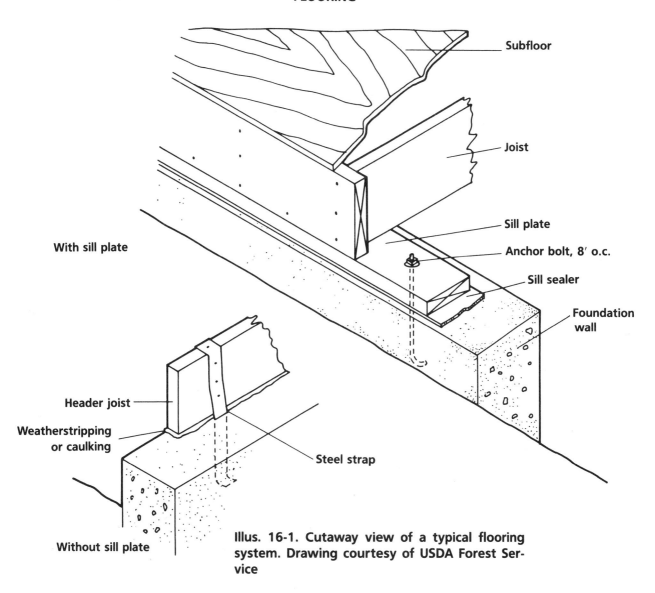

Illus. 16-1. Cutaway view of a typical flooring system. Drawing courtesy of USDA Forest Service

all situations; check with your local building inspector first.

Another option for joists with small areas of damage is a process where the old joist is headed off (Illustrations 16-3, 16-4). To head off a joist, cut out the damaged section. Then joist-size material is used to span the distance between sound joists. The cut end of the damaged joist is attached to the new wood that runs perpendicular to the cut end. This procedure is also used when an opening is needed between floor joists for the passage of chimneys or stairs.

Subflooring

Subflooring is attached to the floor joists. It can be made of boards, but it's usually made from sheets of plywood or particleboard. Most jurisdictions allow two options when installing subflooring. One layer of tongue-and-groove material is allowed, or two layers of standard plywood or particleboard may be used.

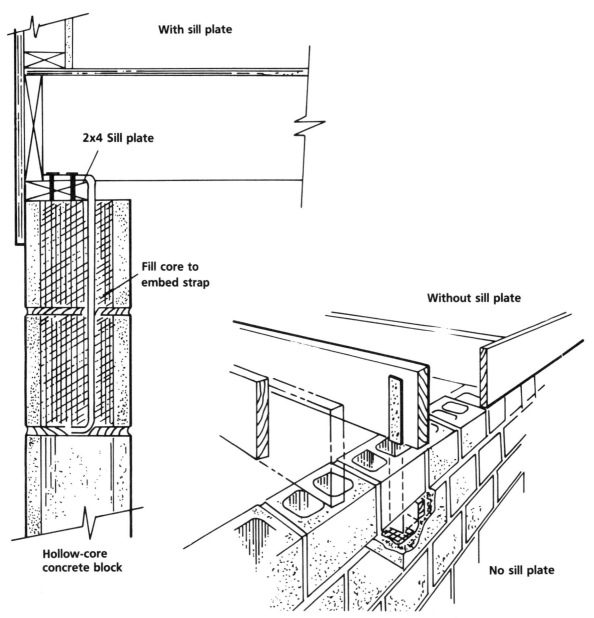

**Illus. 16-2. Floor joist detail. Drawing courtesy of
USDA Forest Service**

Underlayment

Underlayment is usually a thin (about ¼″) sheet of plywood that's laid over a subfloor. The underlayment is normally sanded on one side and provides a smooth surface for installation of finish flooring.

Vinyl Flooring

Vinyl flooring is the most common flooring used in kitchens and bathrooms. It is generally available in widths of six or twelve feet. Vinyl flooring can be tricky to install, but the job can be done by anyone with average skills and patience.

Before you install new vinyl, be sure that the installation area is clean and smooth. The surface should be flat and without cracks, depressions, or bulges. Cracks in floors can be filled with special filling compounds that are available from the same stores that sell flooring.

Before you install the floor, roll up the flooring with the finish side facing outward.

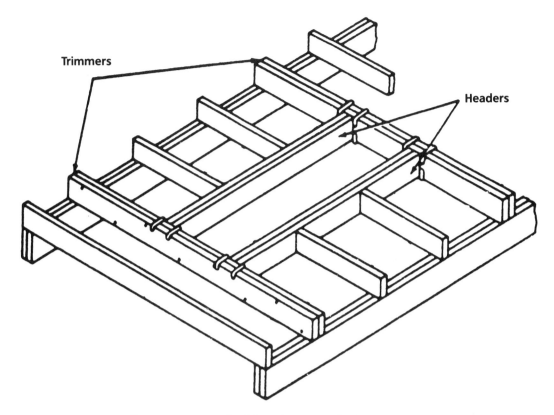

Trimmers

Headers

Illus. 16-3. Detail of headers installed on joists. Drawing courtesy of USDA Forest Service

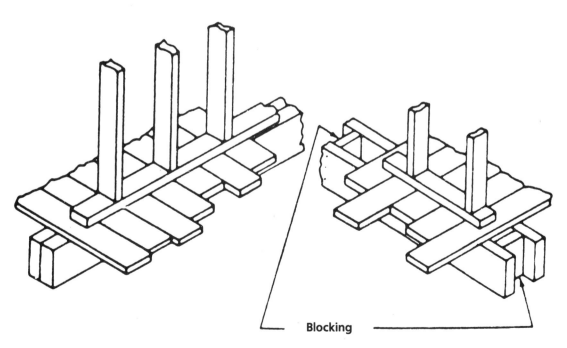

Blocking

Illus. 16-4. Reinforced joists. Drawing courtesy of USDA Forest Service

Leave it in this position for a full day. Maintain an even temperature of about 65°F (19°C) in the room in which the vinyl is stored.

If your floor will require seams, make them before installing the flooring. Lay two pieces of flooring in place so that they overlap. Make sure the pattern meets and matches. Using a straightedge and a utility knife, cut through both pieces of flooring where the seam will be made. Remove the scrap flooring and attach the two pieces of finish flooring to the floor at the seam. Use a hand roller to press the flooring down. The back of the flooring should be in contact with the adhesive or tape you're using. Cover the seam with a sealing compound.

Vinyl flooring should be laid out with enough excess vinyl that the flooring rolls up on the walls. A utility knife is one of the best tools to use to cut vinyl flooring.

When you secure the flooring to the subfloor, you may use adhesive, tape, staples, or a combination of all of these.

A floor roller should be used to roll out wrinkles from new flooring. Rollers can be rented at tool-rental centers. When the vinyl is flat, cut away excess flooring. Run a utility knife along a straightedge to cut the vinyl where it meets the walls. Baseboard or shoe molding will then be installed to hide the joint between the floor and the wall.

Carpet

Carpet isn't a common covering for kitchen and bathroom floors, but it's sometimes used. If you want to install carpeting in your bathroom, weigh the pros and cons. Carpeting will make the floor warmer and less slippery than if you use vinyl or tile, but it retains moisture, and that could create problems with mold, mildew, and rot.

If, after careful consideration, you decide to install carpeting in your bathroom or kitchen, make sure the pile of the carpet faces the entrance; this will enhance the appearance of your room. Most carpet is available in widths up to twelve feet.

Homeowners can install loop-pile and cut-pile carpeting, but they'll probably have to rent a few tools. They'll also have to be careful measuring and cutting.

Most carpet is held in place by tackless strips. These strips are normally about four feet long and have sharp teeth that bite into the carpet. Tackless strips come in different widths. Check with your carpet supplier for the proper size to use with your carpet and pad.

The tackless strips are installed around the perimeter of the area to be carpeted. Doorways and cased openings are fitted with metal trim strips. These strips are either folded over or nailed on top of the carpet to give a finished edge that people won't trip over.

Tackless strips should be installed at a uniform distance from the wall. Check with your carpet supplier to determine the proper distance between the edge of the strip and the wall. As a general rule, keep a gap that's equal to two-thirds the thickness of the carpet.

The carpet pad is installed within the boundaries of the tackless strips, but it isn't attached to the strips. Check the manufacturer's recommendations to determine which side of the pad should face the subfloor. Carpet pads are usually stapled to the subfloor.

Carpeting should be unrolled, flattened out, and stored at room temperature before it's cut. When you do cut the carpet, leave at least three inches of extra carpet in all directions. If you work with cut-pile carpet, cut it from the back. Take measurements and use a utility knife, along with a chalk line or straightedge, to make an even cut along the carpet backing. Loop-pile carpet should be cut on the finished side.

Carpet installation requires the use of a tool that stretches the carpet. There are knee-kickers and power stretchers available for this chore, and both tools can be rented at most tool-rental centers.

Carpet should be seamed (if it needs it) before it's stretched. Two pieces of carpet should overlap each other by about one inch at the seam. Make sure the pile of both pieces of carpet runs in the same direction. Use a row-running knife to cut a straight line along the edge of the overlapped carpet. The knife will cut both pieces of carpet simultaneously.

When the cut is complete, remove the cut strip from beneath the top piece of carpet. Lay back both edges to expose the subfloor.

Install a strip of hot-melt seaming tape on the subfloor. The tape should be laid so that the center of the tape is in line with the center point of where the two pieces of carpet will meet.

Run a hot iron over the seaming tape to activate it. Heat only small sections at a time, and maintain an iron temperature of about 250°F (121°C). When the tape becomes sticky, roll the edges of the carpet into place and butt them together. Continue this process, in small sections, until the complete seam is made.

To stretch carpet, you should have both a knee-kicker and a power stretcher. The stretching process usually begins in a corner. Using the knee-kicker, attach the carpet to the tackless strips on two walls, at corners.

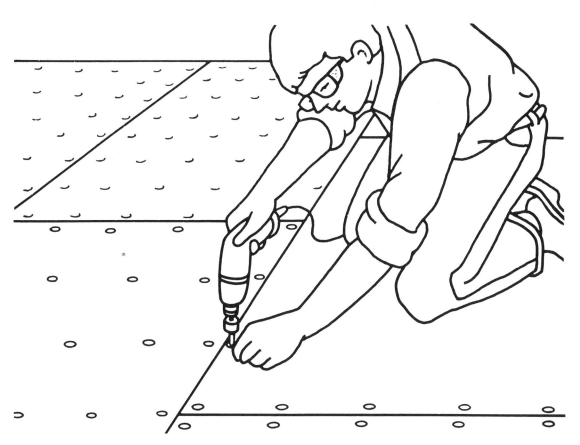

Illus. 16-5. Installing the underlayment on a floor, before laying down the tile. Drawing courtesy of United States Gypsum Company

After the first corner is secured, use a power stretcher to secure the corner directly opposite the corner already done. Power stretchers can telescope out to long lengths, and they can span an entire room.

Knee-kickers are used to secure carpet between previously secured locations. Two walls will be done using the knee-kicker, and two walls will be done using the power stretcher.

When the carpet is attached to the tackless strips, cut away the excess carpet, using a utility knife. Then use a flat-bit screwdriver to tuck any remaining carpet into the gap between the tack strip and the wall.

Carpet at doorways and openings should be cut to size, and a metal strip should then be installed on top of the carpet. If you use a metal strip that must be bent over the carpeting, use a wide block of wood and a hammer to drive the metal strip down tight. The wooden block should be placed over the strip and tapped down with the hammer. Don't hit the strip with just a hammer, or you'll damage the strip. If you use a nail-on strip, simply put the metal in place and tack it down.

Ceramic Tile

Ceramic tile is often found in bathrooms and kitchens (see the color photos on pages 67, 68, 70, 71, 124, and 125). If you decide to use tile, you'll have many choices. Tile floors can be made of quarry tile, mosaic tile, and glazed ceramic tile. Quarry tile comes in large squares, and it comes in natural clay colors. Mosaic tile is small, and generally comes with numerous tiles connected to a single backing. Glazed ceramic tile may be bought as squares or rectangles.

Underlayment should be installed over the subfloor before tile is installed (Illus. 16-5). The underlayment should be at least 3/8″ thick and should be installed with 1/8″ expansion gaps between the sheets. The tile can be secured using adhesives. The adhesive may be organic or epoxy. Epoxy is the preferred adhesive for floors where moisture is a potential problem. The choice of which type of adhesive to use is often determined by the manufacturer's recommendations.

Grout is a product that fills the gaps between tiles, preventing water and dirt from collecting in the voids. There are many types of grout; check with your tile dealer before selecting grout.

Proper planning is a critical element of good tile installation. How to obtain the proper pattern and spacing will require thought. Special cutters (which can be rented at tool-rental centers) should be used to cut tile.

Installation methods vary; check with your dealer and follow the manufacturer's recommendations. Here's one common way to install tile.

Trowel on 1/4″ of adhesive on the underlayment. Use plastic spacers (available at tile dealers) to maintain even spacing between tiles. Lay the first tile in the center of the floor and lay subsequent tiles out from that point.

As you set the tiles in the adhesive, press them down firmly. A rubber hammer can be used to tap the tile into place, but you may not need it. Use a long level to check the consistency of the floor; the tile should be installed level. After the tile is set, wait for the adhesive to dry.

When the adhesive is dry, you'll be ready to grout the tile. The grout should be spread over the floor (usually with a special trowel), filling all gaps between the tiles.

Once the grout has filled the cracks, wash off the excess grout using a wet sponge. To be sure to install the tile properly, follow the tile manufacturer's recommendations.

Illustrations 16-6 through 16-23 show all the steps needed to install ceramic tile. Illustrations 16-24 and 16-25 show two beautifully tiled kitchens.

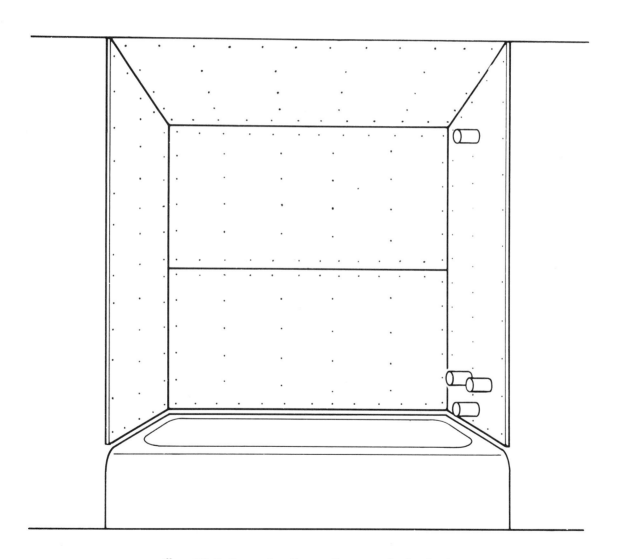

Illus. 16-6. Preparing the walls around a bathtub for tile installation. Drawing courtesy of United States Gypsum Company

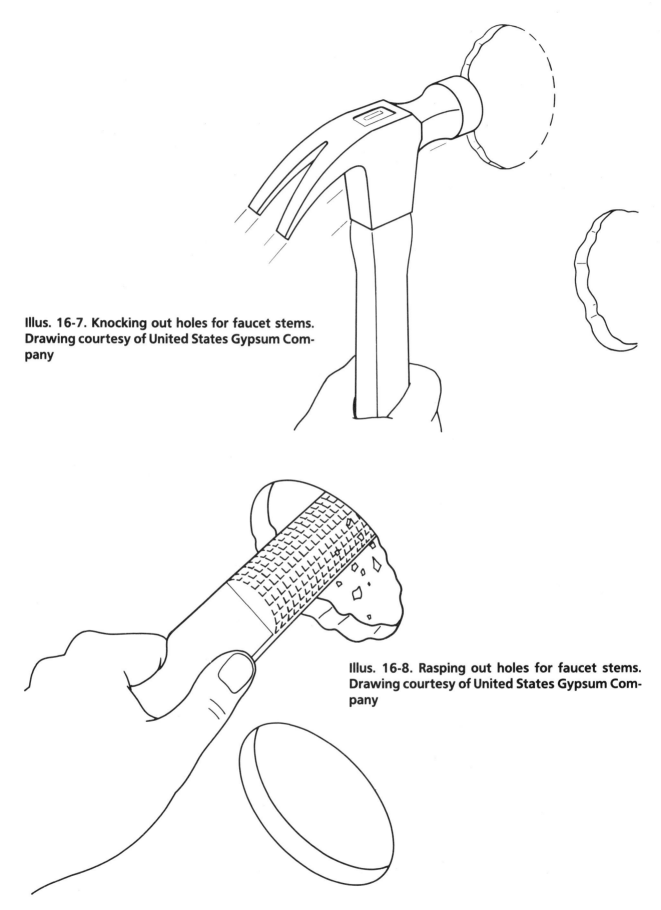

Illus. 16-7. Knocking out holes for faucet stems. Drawing courtesy of United States Gypsum Company

Illus. 16-8. Rasping out holes for faucet stems. Drawing courtesy of United States Gypsum Company

Carriage House, "Vintage II" door, white enamel on maple. Photo courtesy of Plain 'n Fancy Custom Cabinetry

Carriage House, "Serenade II" door, "Salmon" stain on cherry. Photo courtesy of Plain 'n Fancy Custom Cabinetry

Weatherburne, beaded inset, "Cinnamon" on pine. Photo courtesy of Plain 'n Fancy Custom Cabinetry

"Vintage II," "Singleton II" doors, natural stain on oak. Photo courtesy of Plain 'n Fancy Custom Cabinetry

Richland, Coleman & Dover doors, tinted white finish. Photo courtesy of Plain 'n Fancy Custom Cabinetry

Wastebasket pull-out. Photo courtesy of Plain 'n Fancy Custom Cabinetry

Bread drawer with acrylic lid. Photo courtesy of Plain 'n Fancy Custom Cabinetry

"Vintage II" doors, natural stain on oak. Photo courtesy of Plain 'n Fancy Custom Cabinetry

Carriage House, "Reverse-A-Shelf." Photo courtesy of Plain 'n Fancy Custom Cabinetry

Richland tall canned-goods cabinet. Photo courtesy of Plain 'n Fancy Custom Cabinetry

(Above) Richland pie-cut revolving shelf. Photo courtesy of Plain 'n Fancy Custom Cabinetry

(Left) Richland retractable wire garbage basket. Photo courtesy of Plain 'n Fancy Custom Cabinetry

Richland base rack with a pull-out wire shelf. Photo courtesy of Plain 'n Fancy Custom Cabinetry

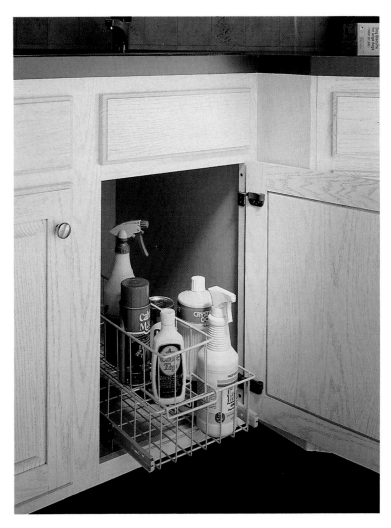

Richland wire under-sink pull-out. Photo courtesy of Plain 'n Fancy Custom Cabinetry

Richland corner revolving shelf. Photo courtesy of Plain 'n Fancy Custom Cabinetry

Richland pull-out shelves. Photo courtesy of Plain 'n Fancy Custom Cabinetry

Toe-kick drawer. Photo courtesy of Plain 'n Fancy Custom Cabinetry

Carriage House burnished-cherry vanity. Photo courtesy of Plain 'n Fancy Custom Cabinetry

(Above) Carriage House, "Elegante II" door in natural walnut. Photo courtesy of Plain 'n Fancy Custom Cabinetry

(Left) Carriage House, "Mirage II" door, "Midnight Blue" laminate and natural wood. Photo courtesy of Plain 'n Fancy Custom Cabinetry

A colorful bathroom. Photo courtesy of Ralph Wilson Plastics Co.

Large, open bathroom. Photo courtesy of Ralph Wilson Plastics Co.

An elegant tiled bathroom. Photo
courtesy of American Olean Tile
Company

A built-in whirlpool bath.
Photo courtesy of Amer-
ican Olean Tile Company

A rich, warm kitchen. Photo courtesy of Wood-Mode, Inc.

A space-saving kitchen. Photo courtesy of Clairson International

A family kitchen. Photo courtesy of Benjamin Moore & Co.

A kitchen with wood flooring, an island, and decorated in light colors. Photo courtesy of Wood-Mode, Inc.

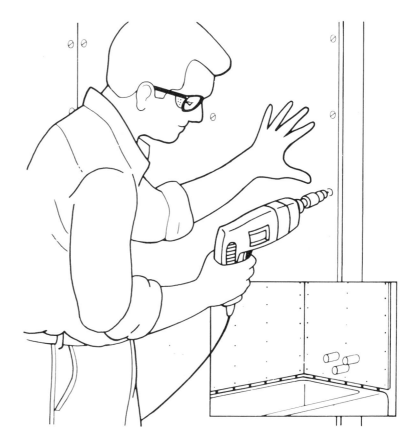

Illus. 16-9. Screwing wallboard backing into the walls surrounding a bathtub. Drawing courtesy of United States Gypsum Company

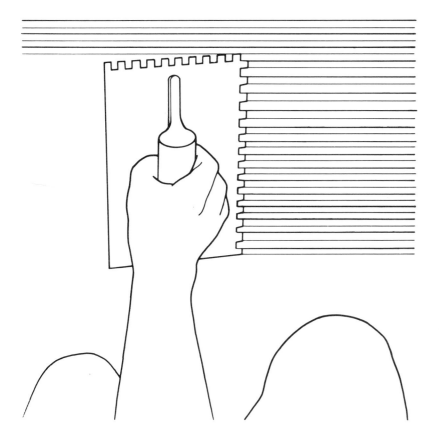

Illus. 16-10. Applying adhesive for tile. Drawing courtesy of United States Gypsum Company

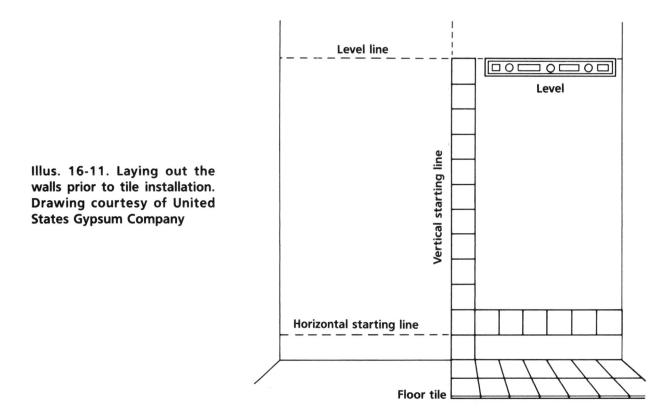

Illus. 16-11. Laying out the walls prior to tile installation. Drawing courtesy of United States Gypsum Company

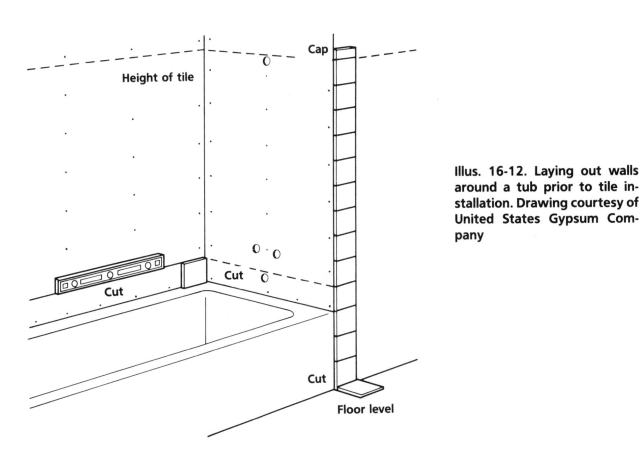

Illus. 16-12. Laying out walls around a tub prior to tile installation. Drawing courtesy of United States Gypsum Company

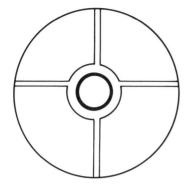

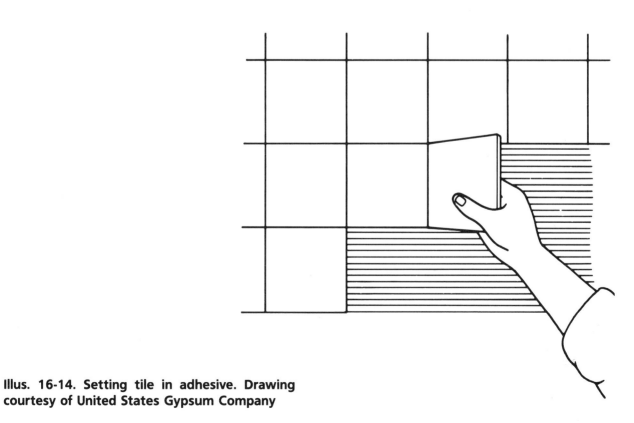

Illus. 16-13. Tile partially laid around a bathtub. Circle is a closet flange for a toilet. Drawing courtesy of United States Gypsum Company

Illus. 16-14. Setting tile in adhesive. Drawing courtesy of United States Gypsum Company

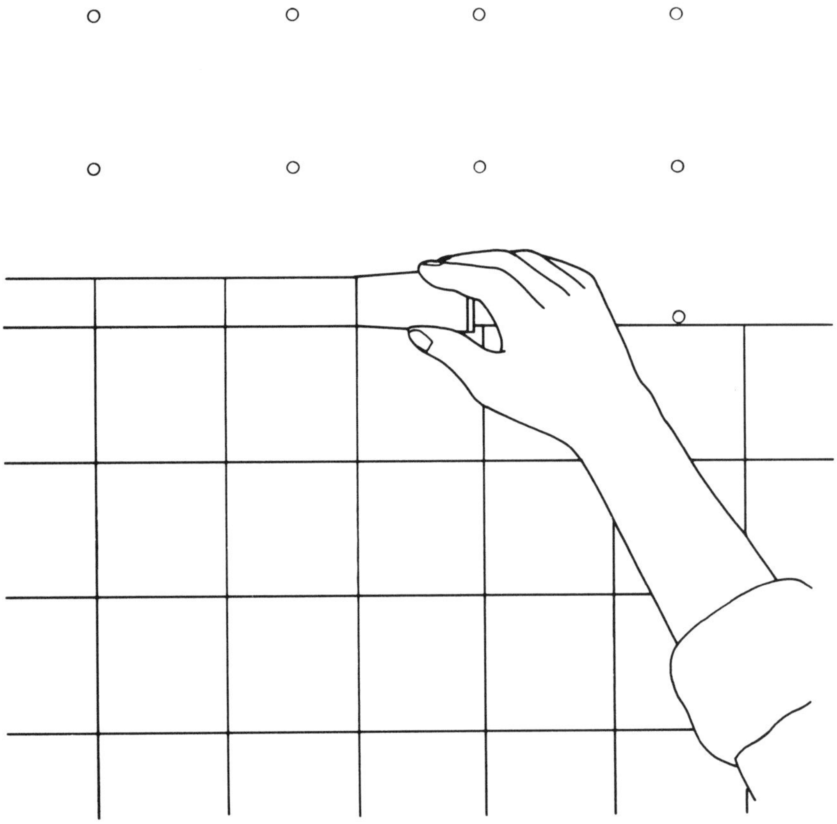

Illus. 16-15. Installing trim tile to finish an edge. Drawing courtesy of United States Gypsum Company

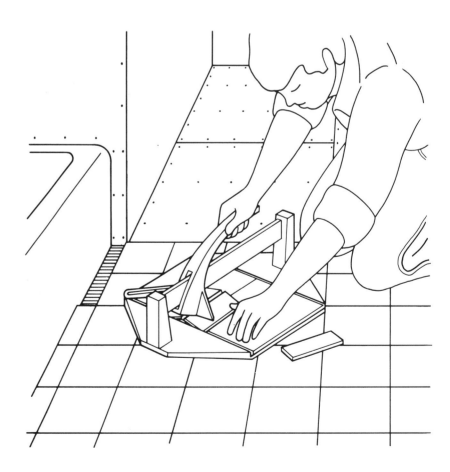

Illus. 16-16. Cutting tile. Drawing courtesy of United States Gypsum Company

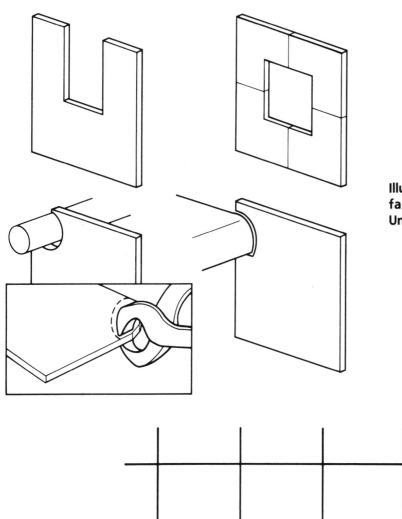

Illus. 16-17. Nipping tile to fit around faucet stems. Drawing courtesy of United States Gypsum Company

Illus. 16-18. Applying grout to tile. Drawing courtesy of United States Gypsum Company

Illus. 16-19. Spreading grout on tile. Drawing courtesy of United States Gypsum Company

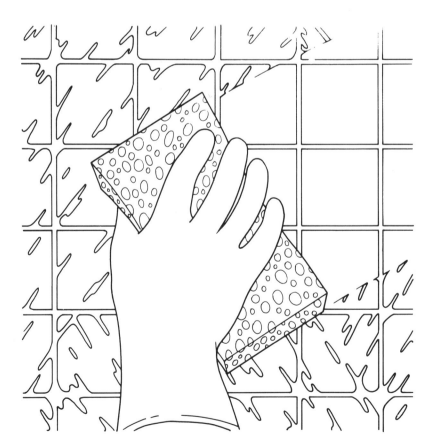

Illus. 16-20. Washing off excess grout from tile. Drawing courtesy of United States Gypsum Company

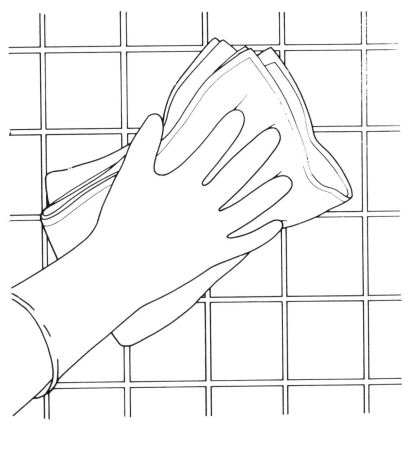

Illus. 16-21. Toweling off the excess grout for a final finish. Drawing courtesy of United States Gypsum Company

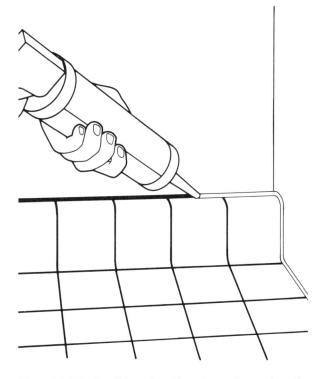

Illus. 16-22. Caulking between the tile edge and the bathtub edge. Drawing courtesy of United States Gypsum Company

Illus. 16-23. Caulking the tile edge where the tile meets the walls. Drawing courtesy of United States Gypsum Company

Illus. 16-24. A tiled kitchen. Photo courtesy of Lis King Public Relations

Illus. 16-25. Another tiled kitchen. Photo courtesy of Lis King Public Relations

17
Walls & Ceilings

Walls and ceilings can account for much of your remodeling work. If finished walls aren't removed, you may just have to paint, but major remodeling often involves building new walls and recovering old walls, requiring considerable effort. The skills of many trades may be needed.

You may have to frame new interior partitions or install a new door or window. You may need to add insulation to the exterior walls. Getting a good finish on drywall is something of an art, and even painting isn't always as easy as it looks.

Framing

Framing is often called "rough" carpentry. If the framing isn't done properly, the rest of the job will suffer. For example, if you frame a new wall and it's out of plumb, you'll have a tough time hanging cabinets satisfactorily. Some kitchen and bathroom remodeling jobs don't require any framing work, but others do. Framing interior partitions isn't difficult, but a few tricks of the trade will make the job easier.

Building a Wall

When you build a wall, you can get the job done in several ways. Most professionals build walls while the framing rests on the subfloor, and then they stand the walls up. This process allows you to frame the entire wall comfortably.

Before you start driving nails (Illustrations 17-1 through 17-3), lay out the wall locations on the subfloor. Mark the wall location with a chalk line. Once the wall location is known, measure the length of the future wall. This process will show you how long the top and bottom (sole) plates (Illus. 17-4) should be.

Carpenters normally use one 2×4 as a bottom plate and two 2×4 studs for the top plate of a wall (Illustrations 17-5, 17-6). Begin by cutting the bottom and top plates to the desired length. Next, measure to determine the length needed for vertical studs. Remember to allow for the thickness of the top and bottom plates when you measure between the ceiling joists and subfloor. After you're sure of your measurements, cut the wall studs to the desired length.

Turn over the bottom and top plates on their edges. Place the first wall stud at one end of the plates and nail it into place. Do the same with a second stud at the other end. You've just created a rectangle, and all you have to do is install the additional wall studs. Studs are normally installed so that there's 16″ from the center of one stud to the center of another. When the wall section is complete, stand it up and nail it into place.

Windows & Doors

Your work may involve framing for windows and doors (Illustrations 17-7 through 17-11). It isn't uncommon for new windows and doors to be installed during large remodeling jobs.

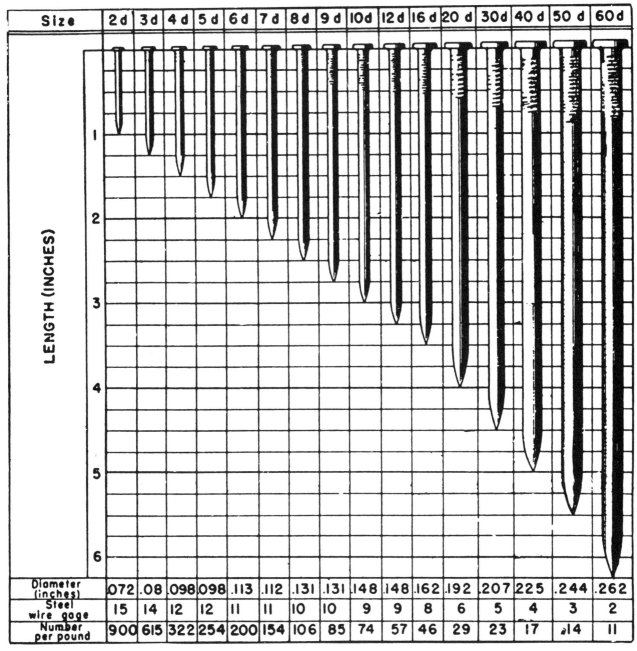

Size	2 d	3 d	4 d	5 d	6 d	7 d	8 d	9 d	10 d	12 d	16 d	20 d	30 d	40 d	50 d	60 d
Diameter (inches)	.072	.08	.098	.098	.113	.112	.131	.131	.148	.148	.162	.192	.207	.225	.244	.262
Steel wire gage	15	14	12	12	11	11	10	10	9	9	8	6	5	4	3	2
Number per pound	900	615	322	254	200	154	106	85	74	57	46	29	23	17	₂14	11

Illus. 17-1. Nail sizes. Chart courtesy of USDA Forest Service

Casement Windows

Casement windows are energy-efficient. Such windows offer full air flow. When you crank out a casement window, the entire window opens.

Double-Hung Windows

Double-hung windows are the windows found in most homes. These windows are generally less expensive than casement windows, and they're well accepted as an industry standard.

Skylights

Skylights can give a kitchen or bathroom plenty of natural light (Illustrations 17-12

Size	Lgth (in.)	Diam (in.)	Remarks	Where used
2d	1	.072	Small head	Finish work, shop work.
2d	1	.072	Large flathead	Small timber, wood shingles, lathes.
3d	1¼	.08	Small head	Finish work, shop work.
3d	1¼	.08	Large flathead	Small timber, wood shingles, lathes.
4d	1½	.098	Small head	Finish work, shop work.
4d	1½	.098	Large flathead	Small timber, lathes, shop work.
5d	1¾	.098	Small head	Finish work, shop work.
5d	1¾	.098	Large flathead	Small timber, lathes, shop work.
6d	2	.113	Small head	Finish work, casing, stops, etc., shop work.
6d	2	.113	Large flathead	Small timber, siding, sheathing, etc., shop work.
7d	2¼	.113	Small head	Casing, base, ceiling, stops, etc.
7d	2¼	.113	Large flathead	Sheathing, siding, subflooring, light framing.
8d	2½	.131	Small head	Casing, base, ceiling, wainscot, etc., shop work.
8d	2½	.131	Large flathead	Sheathing, siding, subflooring, light framing, shop work.
8d	1¼	.131	Extra-large flathead	Roll roofing, composition shingles.
9d	2¾	.131	Small head	Casing, base, ceiling, etc.
9d	2¾	.131	Large flathead	Sheathing, siding, subflooring, framing, shop work.
10d	3	.148	Small head	Casing, base, ceiling, etc., shop work.
10d	3	.148	Large flathead	Sheathing, siding, subflooring, framing, shop work.
12d	3¼	.148	Large flathead	Sheathing, subflooring, framing.
16d	3½	.162	Large flathead	Framing, bridges, etc.
20d	4	.192	Large flathead	Framing, bridges, etc.
30d	4½	.207	Large flathead	Heavy framing, bridges, etc.
40d	5	.225	Large flathead	Heavy framing, bridges, etc.
50d	5½	.244	Large flathead	Extra-heavy framing, bridges, etc.
60d	6	.262	Large flathead	Extra-heavy framing, bridges, etc.

[1] This chart applies to wire nails, although it may be used to determine the length of cut nails.

Illus. 17-2. Recommended uses for nails. Chart courtesy of USDA Forest Service

through 17-15). Rooms filled with sunshine generally appear large and inviting. Skylights are now available with built-in shades and screens.

Metal Doors

Metal doors are relatively inexpensive, and they can be equipped with good insulation. These doors are available as solid doors, solid doors stamped to give the appearance of six-panel doors, and with half of the door being glass, with or without grids. These doors can be painted, but they can't be stained.

Wood Doors

Wood doors, which typically cost more than metal doors, are available in styles not possible with metal doors. Some people don't like wood doors because they warp.

French Doors

These doors are a wonderful way to brighten up an eat-in kitchen. They're beautiful, but expensive.

Framing Window & Door Openings

Framing window and door openings is simple when building new walls, but it can be complicated if you'll be putting new windows or doors into existing walls. Your work will affect the siding on your home and the structural integrity of the exterior wall. Existing conditions in your home may call for professional help during this phase.

A typical window frame will involve jack studs, cripple studs, and a header. The header will provide strength and support for whatever rests atop the wall. It is usually made with lumber that's nailed together.

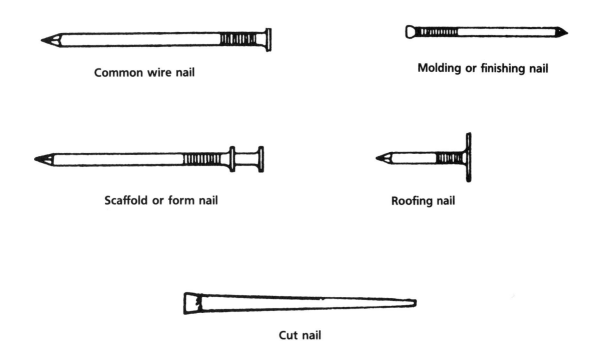

Illus. 17-3. Types of nails. Drawing courtesy of
USDA Forest Service

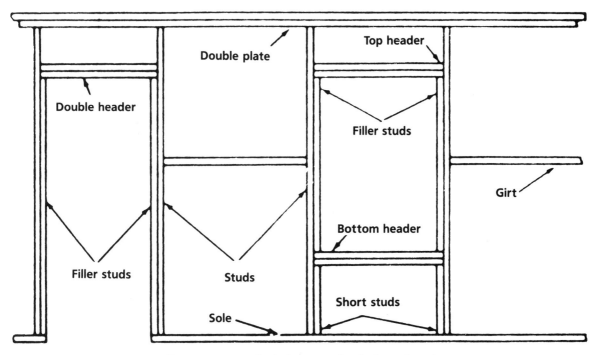

Illus. 17-4. Typical door and window framing.
Drawing courtesy of USDA Forest Service

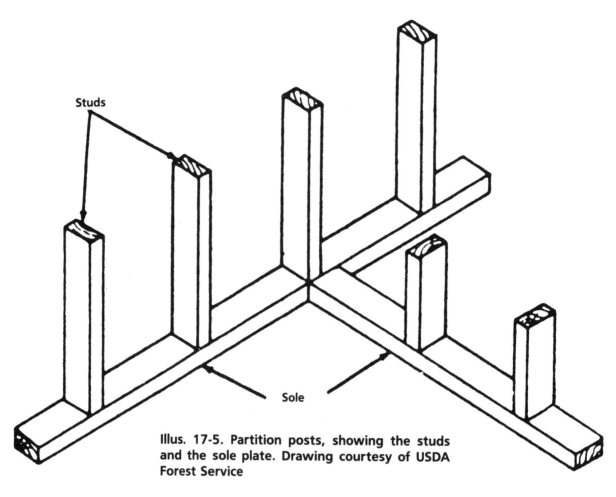

Illus. 17-5. Partition posts, showing the studs and the sole plate. Drawing courtesy of USDA Forest Service

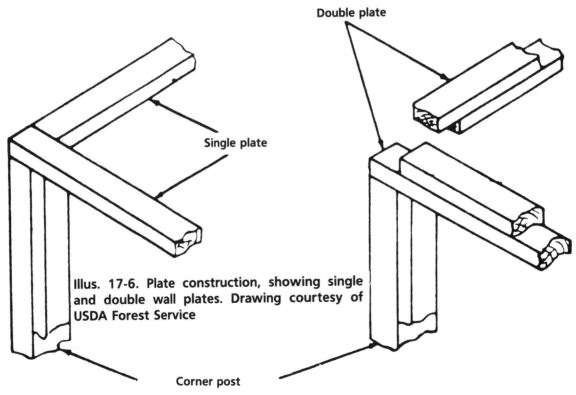

Illus. 17-6. Plate construction, showing single and double wall plates. Drawing courtesy of USDA Forest Service

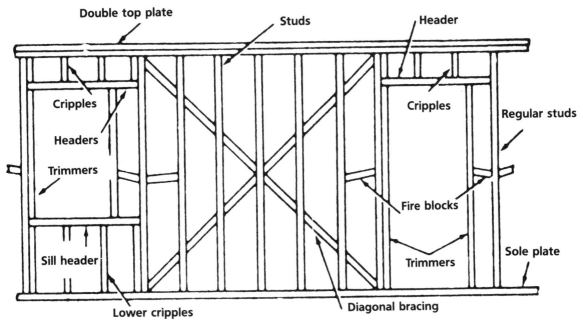

Illus. 17-7. Framing detail. Drawing courtesy of
USDA Forest Service

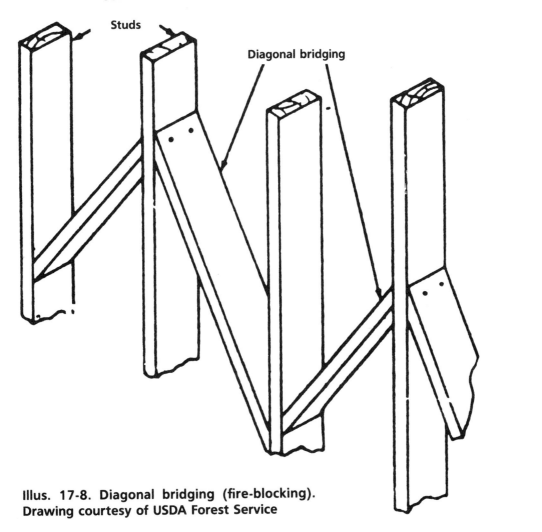

Illus. 17-8. Diagonal bridging (fire-blocking).
Drawing courtesy of USDA Forest Service

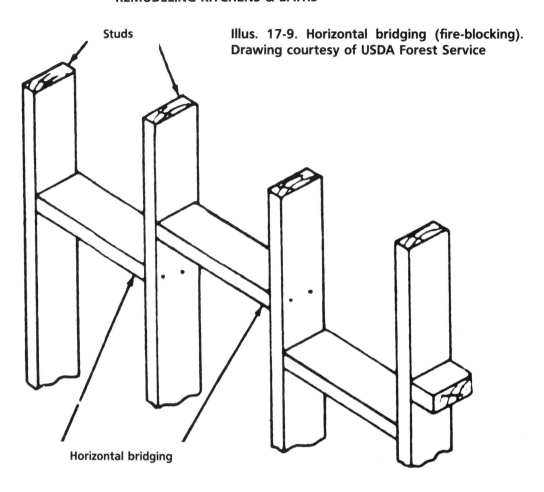

Studs

Illus. 17-9. Horizontal bridging (fire-blocking). Drawing courtesy of USDA Forest Service

Horizontal bridging

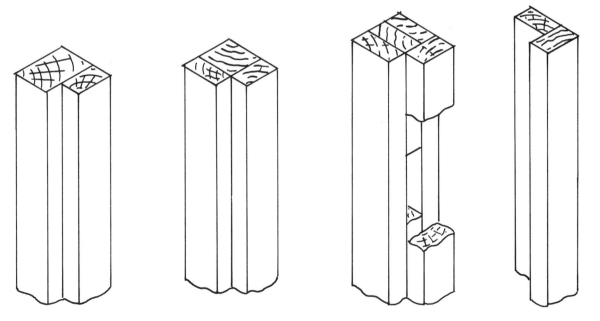

Illus. 17-10. Corner-post construction. Drawing courtesy of USDA Forest Service

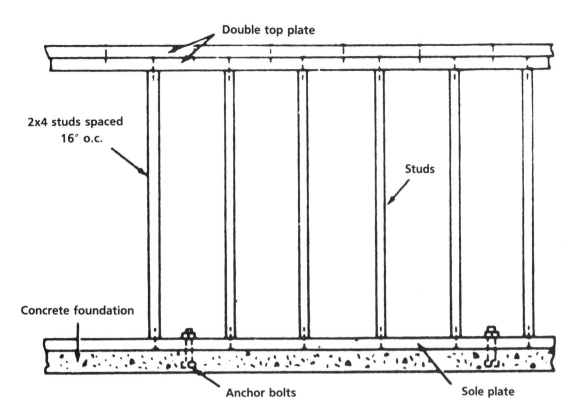

Illus. 17-11. Typical wall-stud placement. Drawing courtesy of USDA Forest Service

Jack studs are installed under the header, and support it. A horizontal board is installed below the header, at a distance equal to the rough-opening dimensions of the window being installed. This board is nailed to the wall studs and supported with short studs, from below. The area above the header is filled with cripple studs. These cripples extend from the header to the top plate, completing the window frame.

Framing for an exterior door is similar to framing for windows. Most doors are available as prehung units, and they arrive at the job ready for installation.

The rough door opening should extend all the way to the subfloor. A header, jack studs, and upper cripples will be installed in a manner very similar to that used for window framing. However, the lower framing (done with a window) is eliminated, and the section of the bottom wall plate that runs through the door opening is cut out.

Window Installation

If you've framed the rough opening properly, window installation should be simple. Most windows have nailing flanges for at-

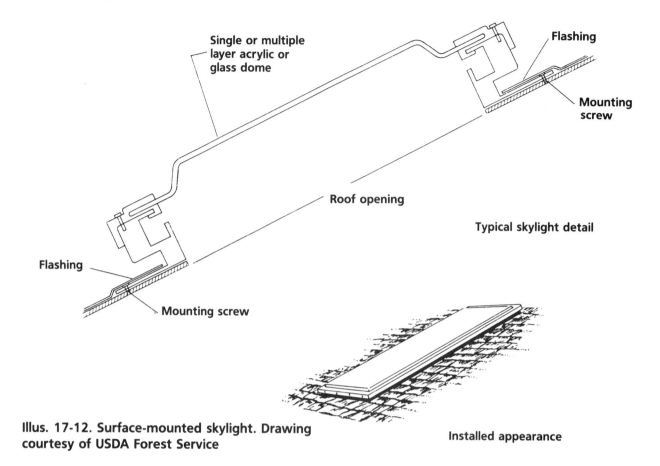

Single or multiple layer acrylic or glass dome

Flashing

Mounting screw

Roof opening

Typical skylight detail

Flashing

Mounting screw

Installed appearance

Illus. 17-12. Surface-mounted skylight. Drawing courtesy of USDA Forest Service

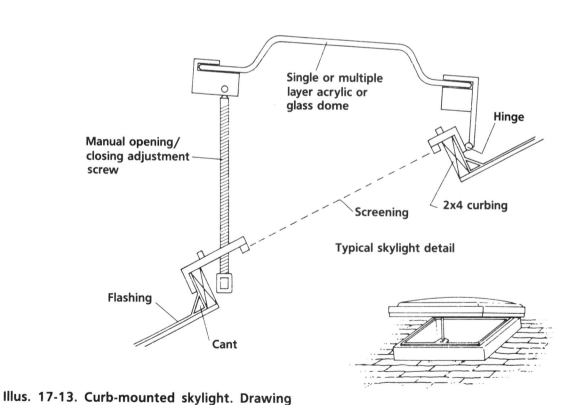

Single or multiple layer acrylic or glass dome

Manual opening/ closing adjustment screw

Hinge

Screening

2x4 curbing

Typical skylight detail

Flashing

Cant

Installed appearance

Illus. 17-13. Curb-mounted skylight. Drawing courtesy of USDA Forest Service

**Illus. 17-14. Skylights in a kitchen/dining area.
Photo courtesy of Lis King Public Relations**

Illus. 17-15. A motorized tool used for opening skylights. Photo courtesy of Velux-America, Inc.

taching the window unit to the frame walls. Set the window unit into the rough opening and make sure it's plumb. Nail the unit in place by driving nails through the flange. The flange should be on the exterior of the house.

Door Installation

When you work with a prehung door, installation isn't difficult. Put the unit in place and level it. It may be necessary to install shims around the frame to get the unit plumb. When the door is plumb, nail the jamb to the framed opening. Whatever you're installing, always read and follow the recommendations from the manufacturer of the product.

Insulation

Insulation (Illustrations 17-16 through 17-20) isn't difficult to install, but it can irritate your skin. The easiest type of insulation to install is batt insulation, which is available in widths made to fit the standard dimensions of wall and joist cavities.

Wall insulation should have a vapor barrier. The barrier should be installed so that it is between the heated room and the insulation. You can buy rolls of batt insulation with a vapor barrier already attached, or you can use unfaced insulation and install sheets of plastic as a vapor barrier. A strong stapler is the only tool needed for installing insulation.

Drywall

Except for its weight, drywall isn't difficult to hang. Finishing it, however, takes some time and practice. When remodeling a bathroom, new moisture-resistant drywall should be used.

Drywall is available in different sizes. Professionals often use 4'×12' sheets to reduce the number of seams in the job, but 4'×8' sheets are much easier for the average person to handle. You can choose from different thicknesses to give your finished wall the proper depth.

Drywall can be hung using nails or screws. Screws are less likely to work loose than nails. If screws are used, an electric screwdriver makes the job go quickly. Screws should be driven tight, to make a depression in the wallboard. When nails are used, they should be driven extra deep, to create a dimple in the drywall. The depressions will be filled with joint compound to hide the nail or screw heads.

Drywall can be cut using a drywall saw, jigsaw, or a utility knife; most professionals use utility knives (Illus. 17-21). Score the drywall with the utility knife, and then break it at the scored seam. Use a T-square, a piece of lumber, or a chalk line to make straight cuts.

Hanging drywall on a ceiling is the most (physically) difficult part of any drywall job. Ceilings should be done before the walls are covered. When you drywall a ceiling, you'll have to make cut-outs for ceiling-mounted electrical boxes. Due to its weight, drywall isn't easy to install above your head. However, there is a way to reduce this burden.

A T-brace helps to hang drywall on a ceiling. You can make a T-brace from scrap studs by nailing a 2×4 (about three feet long) onto the end of a 2×4 that's long enough to reach the ceiling, with a little left over.

The brace can be wedged under drywall to hold it to the ceiling. The T-arm will rest under the drywall and the long section of the brace will be wedged between the subfloor and the ceiling. It normally takes two people to raise drywall to the ceiling joists. Once the T-brace is wedged into place, it frees one of the people up to attach the drywall to the joists. Two braces can be used to free all hands for other work.

It's possible to hang a ceiling by yourself. Rest the drywall on the tops of two ladders.

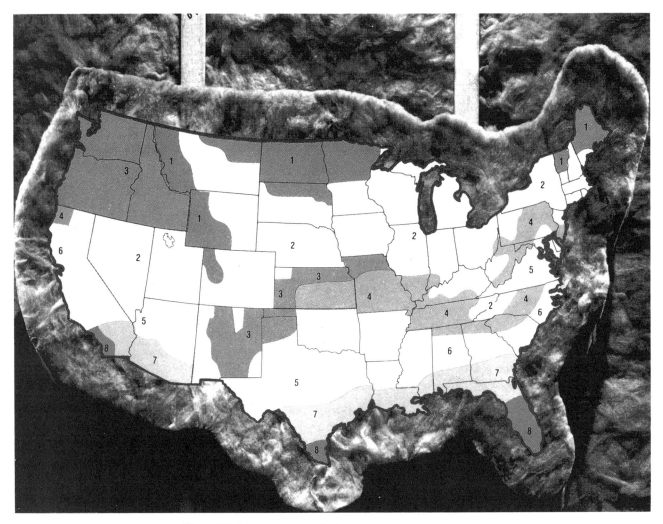

Illus. 17-16. A map of the continental United States, showing recommended insulation-installation zones. Map courtesy of Owens-Corning

Leave a couple of feet of the wallboard hanging over each end of the ladders. Put one T-brace under one end of the drywall and raise that end with the brace. Wedge the brace against the floor and raise the other end of the drywall with another brace. This will take some time and practice, but once you get the hang of it, you'll be able to install your ceiling without help.

Hanging drywall on walls is much easier than it is on ceilings. The drywall can be hung vertically or horizontally (Illus. 17-22). If you hang drywall vertically, you shouldn't need any help. Hanging the dry-wall horizontally generally results in fewer seams, but it's more difficult to do without a helper. There are, however, some tricks that make horizontal hanging easier for the lone remodeler.

Nail large nails to the studs to provide temporary support for the drywall panel. You can then rest the sheet of drywall on the nails while you attach it to the studs. The large nails can be removed once the drywall is secured.

A ledger can be used in place of nails for a more uniform support of the drywall. Nail a 2×4 horizontally across the wall studs.

U.S. DEPARTMENT OF ENERGY RECOMMENDED TOTAL R-VALUES FOR EXISTING HOUSES IN 8 INSULATION ZONES.[A] Map developed by Oakridge National Laboratory from D.O.E. data.					
INSULATION ZONE	CEILINGS BELOW VENTILATED ATTICS		FLOORS OVER UNHEATED CRAWLSPACES, BASEMENTS	(B) NEW CONSTRUCTION EXTERIOR WALLS†	(C) CRAWLSPACE WALLS
	ELECTRIC RESISTANCE	GAS, OIL OR HEAT PUMP	ALL FUEL TYPES		
1	R-49	R-49	R-19	R-19	R-19
2	R-49	R-38	R-19	R-19	R-19
3	R-38	R-38	R-19	R-19	R-19
4	R-38	R-38	R-19	R-19	R-19
5	R-38	R-30	R-19	R-19	R-19
6	R-38	R-30	R-19	R-19	R-19
7	R-30	R-30	(D)	R-19	R-19
8	R-30	R-19	(D)	R-19	R-11

(A) These recommendations are based on the assumption that no structural modifications are needed to accommodate the added insulation.

(B) For new construction, R-19 is recommended for exterior walls. Jamming an R-19 batt into a 3 1/2-inch cavity will not yield R-19.

(C) Insulate crawlspace walls only if the crawlspace is dry all year, the floor above is not insulated, and all ventilation to the crawlspace is blocked. A vapor barrier (e.g. 4- or 6-mil polyethylene film) should be installed on the ground to reduce moisture migration into the crawlspace.

(D) Thermal response of existing space for cooling benefits does not suggest additional insulation.

NOTE: For more information see: D.O.E. Insulation Fact Sheet (D.O.E./CE-0180).

U.S. Department of Energy,
Technical Information Center,
P.O. Box 62, Oak Ridge, TN 37830

†**NOTE:** The D.O.E. recommends an R-19 wall for new construction exterior walls.

An R-19 wall may be achieved by either cavity insulation or a combination of cavity insulation and insulating sheathing.

For 2 x 4 walls, Owens-Corning recommends using either 3 1/2" thick R-15 or 3 1/2" thick R-13 *Fiberglas* insulation with insulated sheathing.

For 2 x 6 walls, Owens-Corning recommends using either 5 1/2" thick R-21 or 6 1/4" thick R-19 *Fiberglas* insulation.

Illus. 17-17. Recommended R-values for insulation. Chart courtesy of Owens-Corning

Rest the drywall on the ledger while you attach it to the studs.

When hanging drywall on the wall studs, don't forget to leave cut-outs for electrical boxes, water supplies, drain arms, and other items that shouldn't be covered up.

Outside corners of walls covered with drywall should be fitted with metal corner bead. These metal strips protect the exposed corners and edges. These strips are perforated and can be nailed or screwed to wall studs. Corner bead is designed to retain joint compound for a smooth finish (Illus. 17-23).

Inside corners don't require metal corner bead. Drywall tape should be creased and installed to cover the seams of these corners.

Taping the seams of new drywall isn't difficult, but it may take some time to develop real expertise. Buy premixed joint compound. The tape you'll be using to cover the seams doesn't have an adhesive backing; it's held in place by the joint compound. Use a wide (about 4″) putty knife to spread the joint compound over the tape, seams, and dimples.

The first coat of joint compound should be spread over seams, corner bead, and dimples; cover one seam at a time. This first coat should be about 3″ wide, and it should be applied generously.

Once the compound covers a seam, lay a strip of tape on the compound, and use a putty knife to work the tape down into the joint compound. The tape should sink deep into the compound. Smooth out the compound and feather it away at the edges of the tape. Continue this process on all the seams.

Tape isn't necessary when filling nail dimples or when covering corner bead. Simply

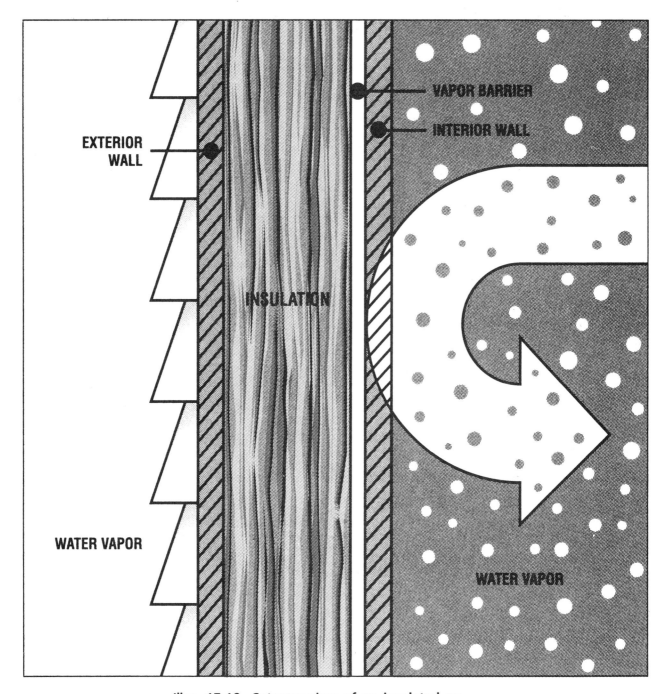

EXTERIOR WALL

INSULATION

WATER VAPOR

VAPOR BARRIER

INTERIOR WALL

WATER VAPOR

Illus. 17-18. Cutaway view of an insulated exterior wall. Drawing courtesy of Owens-Corning

apply joint compound in the depressions until the compound is flush with the drywall. Smooth out the compound with your putty knife, and then let the compound dry.

The first layer of joint compound should dry within 24 hours. A second layer will be applied atop the first layer, about twice as wide as the first layer. The second layer should be left to dry, usually within 24 hours. A third layer of compound is usually the final finish. Before applying the last coat of compound, sand the second coat.

Sand the compound, first with a medium-grit sandpaper, and then with fine-grit. A

R-VALUE	THICKNESS	WIDTH	SQ. FT./PACKAGE
SQUARE FOOTAGE PER PINK FIBERGLAS® INSULATION PACKAGE			
KRAFT PAPER FACED — ROLL PRODUCTS			
R-19	6 1/4"	15"	48.96
R-19	6 1/4"	23"	75.07
R-13	3 1/2"	15"	88.12
R-11	3 1/2"	15"	88.12
R-11	3 1/2"	23"	135.12
UNFACED — ROLL PRODUCTS			
R-25	8"	15"	22.50
R-25	8"	23"	34.50
R-19	6 1/4"	15"	48.96
R-19	6 1/4"	23"	75.07
R-19	6 1/4"	15 1/4"	48.96
R-19	6 1/4"	23 1/4"	75.07
R-13	3 1/2"	15 1/4"	88.12
R-11	3 1/2"	15 1/4"	88.12
KRAFT PAPER FACED — BATTS-IN-BAGS PRODUCTS			
R-38	12"	16"	42.66
R-38	12"	24"	64.00
R-38C	10 1/4"	15 1/2"	41.33
R-38C	10 1/4"	23 3/4"	63.33
R-30	9 1/2"	16"	58.67
R-30	9 1/2"	24"	80.00
R-30C	8 1/4"	15 1/2"	56.84
R-30C	8 1/4"	23 5/8"	78.75
R-21	5 1/2"	15"	67.81
R-21	5 1/2"	23"	89.12
R-19	6 1/4"	15"	77.50
R-19	6 1/4"	23"	118.83
R-15	3 1/2"	15"	67.81
R-15	3 1/2"	23"	103.97
R-13	3 1/2"	15"	125.94
R-11	3 1/2"	15"	155.00
R-11	3 1/2"	23"	237.67
UNFACED — BATTS-IN-BAGS PRODUCTS			
R-38	12"	16"	42.67
R-38	12"	24"	64.00
R-38C	10 1/4"	15 1/2"	41.33
R-38C	10 1/4"	23 3/4"	63.33
R-30	9 1/2"	16"	58.67
R-30	9 1/2"	24"	80.00
R-21	5 1/2"	15"	67.81
R-21	5 1/2"	23"	89.12
R-19	6 1/4"	15 1/4"	77.50
R-19	6 1/4"	23 1/4"	118.83
R-15	3 1/2"	15"	67.81
R-15	3 1/2"	23"	103.97
R-13	3 1/2"	15 1/4"	125.94
R-11	3 1/2"	15 1/4"	155.00

Illus. 17-19. Specifications for various insulation products. Chart courtesy of Owens-Corning

NUMBER OF INSULATION PACKAGES NEEDED FOR COMMON ATTIC DIMENSIONS

R-25 (8" Thick/23" Wide) Attic Blanket® Fiberglas® Insulation

Attic Dimensions	24' x 20'	24' x 40'	30' x 40'
Square Feet To Be Insulated	480	960	1200
Square Feet Per Package	34.50	34.50	34.50
Number of Packages Needed	14 rolls	28 rolls	35 rolls

NUMBER OF INSULATION PACKAGES NEEDED PER WALL

R-13 (3 1/2" Thick/15" Wide) Fiberglas® Insulation

Individual Wall Dimensions	8' x 10'	8' x 15'	8' x 25'
Square Feet To Be Insulated††	80	120	200
Square Feet Per Package	88.12	88.12	88.12
Number of Packages Needed Per Wall	1 roll	2 rolls	3 rolls

††Deduct window and door areas (in square feet) for each wall.

NUMBER OF INSULATION PACKAGES NEEDED FOR COMMON FLOOR DIMENSIONS

R-19 (6 1/4" Thick/15" Wide) Fiberglas® Insulation

Individual Floor Dimensions	16' x 16'	16' x 20'	16' x 30'
Square Feet To Be Insulated	256	320	480
Square Feet Per Package	48.96	48.96	48.96
Number of Packages Needed	6 rolls	7 rolls	10 rolls

Illus. 17-20. Insulation estimating guide. Chart courtesy of Owens-Corning

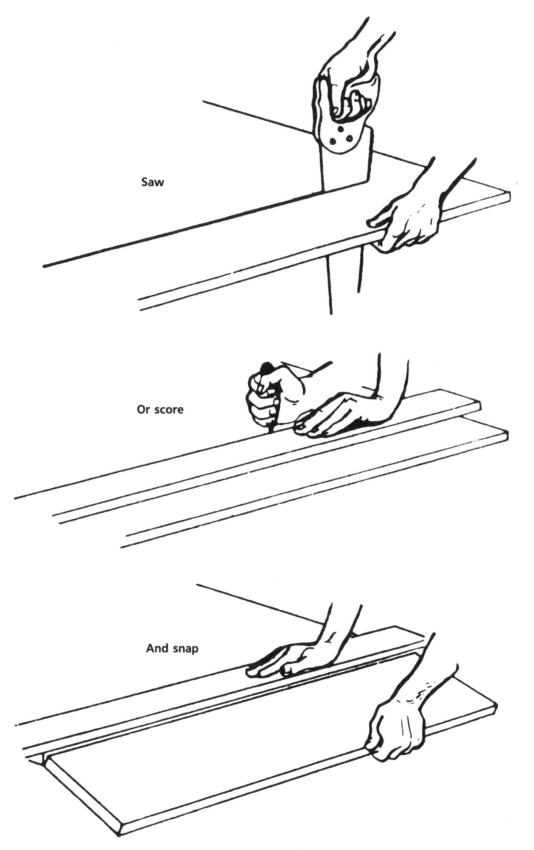

Saw

Or score

And snap

Illus. 17-21. Methods used to cut drywall. Drawing courtesy of USDA Forest Service

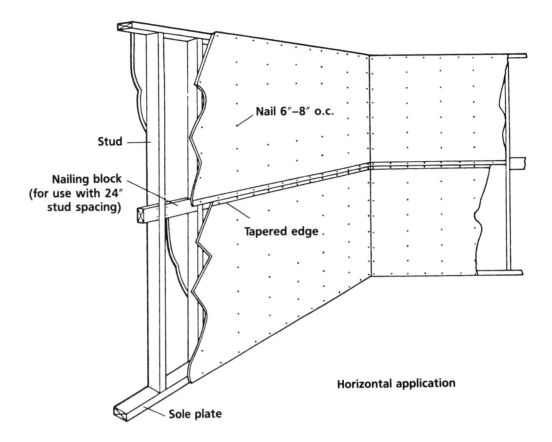

Nail 6″–8″ o.c.

Stud

Nailing block
(for use with 24″
stud spacing)

Tapered edge

Horizontal application

Sole plate

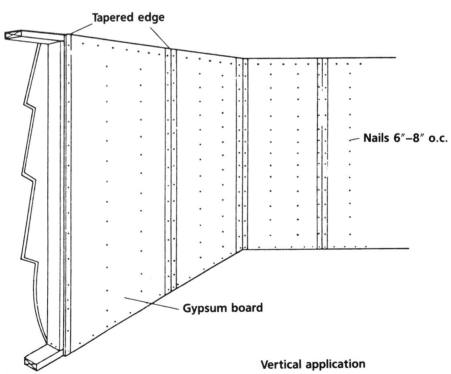

Tapered edge

Nails 6″–8″ o.c.

Gypsum board

Vertical application

Illus. 17-22. Vertical and horizontal installation methods for drywall. Drawing courtesy of USDA Forest Service

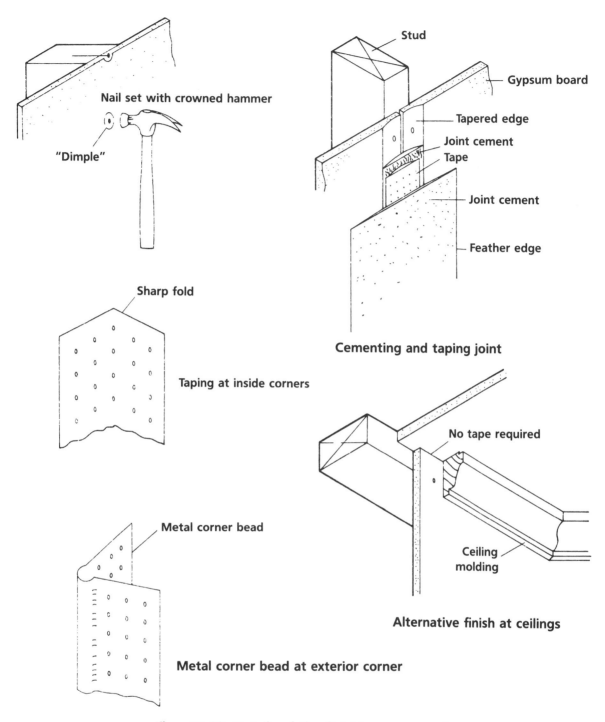

Illus. 17-23. Details of the finishing process of drywall installation. Drawing courtesy of USDA Forest Service

good dust mask is very helpful during this job. A sanding block will make the job go faster and will be easier on your hands than just using sandpaper sheets. Sand the compound with soft strokes to avoid scarring the walls.

When the second layer of compound has been sanded properly, apply the third layer of compound. This last layer should be a thin coat, about 10″ wide, and the edges should be feathered out.

After the final coat has dried, it must be sanded. Use fine-grit sandpaper for the finish sanding. When this step is complete, you are ready to clean up and prepare to prime and paint the walls.

Some will install baseboards and other trim at this time, but others will wait until the cabinets are installed. Installation of interior trim is covered in chapter 19.

Paint

Before you begin to paint, vacuum the room to remove all dust. If you don't vacuum, the paint will catch the dust, and the job won't look good. You'll be working over a subfloor, so dropcloths aren't necessary.

Should you use latex or oil paint? Latex cleans up better than oil, and it will do a fine job on your walls and ceilings. New walls and ceilings should receive at least one coat of primer and one coat of paint. When buying your primer, ask the paint dealer to tint it to match the finish color.

Most painters begin with the ceilings. Paint rollers work well for applying paint and primer to ceilings. If you paint a ceiling with a roller, you'll have to use a brush to cut in along the joints between the walls and ceiling. Use a 2″ or 3″ brush to apply a strip of paint to the edges of the ceiling. As soon as the strip of wet paint is applied, lay down the brush and pick up a roller. Use an extension handle in the roller to avoid numerous trips up and down a ladder.

Roll paint on the ceiling and over the strip of fresh paint. Do the cut-in work a little at a time. Trying to cut in the whole ceiling before rolling on the paint will result in a mismatched finish. The cut-in strips will dry before the rest of the paint does. This results in two different finishes and looks strange. Roll paint on the ceiling in generous amounts; otherwise, the paint will dry without covering the surface.

With the ceiling finished, you'll be ready to paint the walls. Apply cut-in strips of fresh paint around the tops of the walls. Follow the same procedures you used on the ceiling to avoid mismatched paint.

After the first coat of paint or primer, you may see imperfections that had been invisible. Take time between the first and second coat to touch up the drywall. Vacuum any dust created from the touch-up work before applying the second coat of paint.

You may wish to *texture* your ceiling. If you do, there are many options available. Joint compound (what you used to finish drywall) can be used to create a textured ceiling. Some types of textured paint are sold.

A variety of devices can be used to texture a ceiling. A stiff paint brush can be used to create texture, as can a stipple paint roller. Trowels can be used, and even potato mashers are used to texture ceilings.

Trim around windows, doors, and walls will also need to be painted or stained. Gloss-finish paint is used on trim when matte-finish paint is used on walls. Kitchen and bathroom walls are often painted with gloss paint; it's easier to clean than flat paint.

Before the final paint or stain can be applied to trim, fill nail holes with putty. Wood putty and a small putty knife are all that are needed for this job. If you stain the trim, use a putty that won't show through the stain.

Trim is often stained or painted before it's installed. If you'll be staining trim, be sure to get clear wood for the trim material. Trim can be stained using either a staining mitt or a brush.

After the trim has been stained, you may wish to apply a sealer over the stain. This isn't required, but some people prefer the look and durability of sealants.

18
Mechanical Modifications

Some mechanical modifications are generally required in all kitchen and bathroom remodeling jobs. Not all renovations and alterations are big jobs, but they can be. Even minor modifications can present major problems for the inexperienced.

A plumbing connection that isn't made properly may blow apart, flooding the room being remodeled, and (perhaps) the rest of the house. A mix-up in electrical wiring can be difficult to locate and can cause a number of problems. Moving a floor register to gain better heating can result in serious cuts from the sharp metal used in duct work.

Little jobs can create big problems. Most of the problems can be avoided, and many of them are easy to correct, but you must know how to avoid and correct mechanical problems.

Plumbing Pipes Used for Drains & Vents

Many types of plumbing pipes are used for drains and vents. Most modern plumbing uses plastic pipe, but older homes may have cast-iron pipes, galvanized steel, brass, lead, or some other type. Some of these pipes don't perform well after time. If you open your walls during remodeling, it may pay to replace sections of your plumbing to avoid future problems.

Cast-Iron Pipe

Cast-iron pipe can be found in houses of all ages. It has not been used extensively in residential plumbing since the mid 1970s,

but it's still used today. If your home is more than twenty years old, there's a good chance that you have cast-iron drains and vents.

While cast-iron was typically used for large drains and vents, galvanized-steel pipe was often used in conjunction with cast-iron for small drains, like those found in kitchen sinks, bathtubs, and lavatories. You'll most likely encounter galvanized steel pipe in simple remodeling jobs.

Cast-iron joints were once made with oakum and molten lead, and they still are today. However, modern technology uses special rubber adapters for making connections with cast iron. There are three basic types of rubber adapters; one resembles a doughnut and is placed in the hub of one pipe so that the end of another pipe can be inserted, making a watertight joint. The other two types are used with cast-iron pipe that doesn't have hubs. These adapters slide over the ends of two pipes and are held in place with stainless-steel clamps. Not only is this type of connection easy to make, it's also safer than working with hot lead.

Unless you'll be relocating a toilet, or altering the main drainage and vent system in your home, it's unlikely that you'll have to work with cast-iron pipe. But since you may wish to relocate a toilet or do some other type of plumbing remodeling, let's take a quick look at how you can simplify such a task.

If you plan to cut cast-iron pipe, go to a tool-rental store and rent a rachet-type soil-pipe cutter. These tools make quick, easy work of cutting cast-iron pipe. All you have to do is to wrap a special cutting chain around the pipe, secure the cutter, and pump the handle a few times, and the pipe is cut cleanly. This is much easier than sawing your way through the pipe with a hacksaw.

Cutting vertical sections of cast-iron pipe can be dangerous. If the pipe isn't supported properly, the vertical piping could come crashing down on you. Before you cut a vertical pipe, make sure it's supported in a way that will protect you.

If you want to convert a piece of cast-iron pipe to another type of pipe (such as plastic), use a universal rubber adapter for the conversion. This will make the job fast and simple.

Galvanized-Steel Pipe

If you have cast-iron pipe in your home, you probably have some galvanized-steel pipe, too. This pipe tends to rust and build up blockages in itself over the years. If you have the opportunity to replace galvanized pipe with plastic pipe, do it. You'll save yourself from future trouble.

Galvanized pipe can be cut with a hacksaw, and the same rubber adapters used to join cast-iron and plastic pipe can be used on galvanized pipe.

DWV Copper

DWV copper was a popular drain and vent pipe for many years, and it's still found in many older homes. Copper drains and vents give very good service, and they shouldn't need to be replaced.

Copper drains and vents can be cut with a hacksaw, and the same universal adapters used with cast-iron and galvanized pipe can be used to convert copper to plastic.

Schedule-Forty Plastic Pipe

Schedule-forty plastic pipe is the drain and vent pipe most often used in modern plumbing. There are two types of schedule-forty plastic pipe used in homes: ABS and PVC. ABS is black and PVC is white.

Both of these pipes are easy to work with, and either of them can be cut with a hacksaw or a standard carpenter's saw. Joints for these pipes are normally made with a solvent or glue. Most plumbing codes recommend a cleaner be used on plastic pipe, and such codes may require that a primer be applied prior to gluing a joint. These pipes can be joined with universal rubber adapters to any of the other types of drains and vents mentioned.

Plumping Pipes for Potable Water

Just as there are a number of approved drain and vent materials, there are also many types of plumbing pipes used for potable (drinking) water.

Copper

Copper water pipes and tubing are the most common water distribution pipes. Copper is a dependable material that provides years of service.

Copper can be cut with a hacksaw, but roller-cutters will cut the pipe much more smoothly. Joints for copper pipes and tubing are usually made by soldering. This can be a problem for some homeowners. Learning to solder watertight joints takes some time and experience. One way to avoid soldering is to use compression fittings, which are available in all shapes and sizes. They're easy to install, and they usually won't leak. If you conceal plumbing in a wall, compression fittings may not be a good idea, but they work great under sinks and in other accessible places. There's some risk that the fittings will develop leaks as the pipes vibrate with use. The leaks will be small and can be corrected easily if they're visible. If plumbing is concealed in a wall, a small leak could go unnoticed for a long time, causing serious damage to the building.

CPVC

CPVC pipe is another alternative for home-owners lacking soldering skills. CPVC is a rigid plastic pipe that's assembled with solvent joints. A cleaner and primer should be used on the pipe and fittings before gluing the joints.

CPVC can be cut quite easily with a hacksaw, and it's simple to install. Allow plenty of time for joints to dry before moving the pipe. If a fresh joint is bumped or twisted before the glue has dried, a leak is likely.

Polybutylene

Polybutylene pipe, a flexible plastic pipe, can be installed much like electrical wiring. The pipe can be snaked through studs, and its flexibility minimizes the number of joints needed.

If you choose polybutylene pipe, you'll have to rent a special crimping tool. Don't

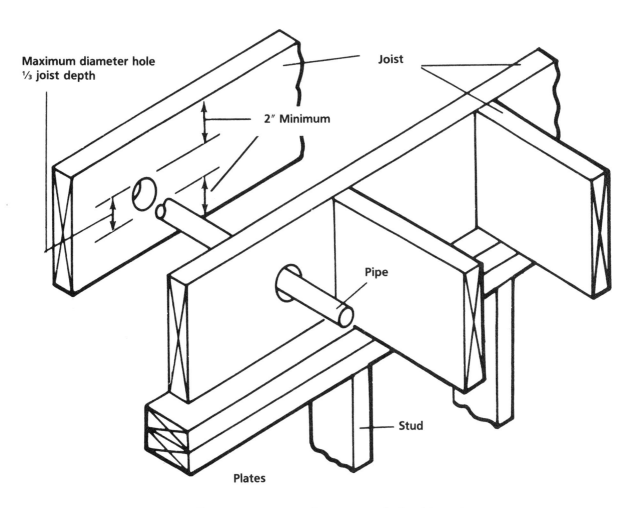

Illus. 18-1. Proper placement of plumbing pipes in floor joists. Drawing courtesy of USDA Forest Service

Illus. 18-2. Cabinet organizers for a bathroom
vanity. Photo courtesy of Clairson International

attempt to make joints with standard stainless-steel clamps. Polybutylene joints require the use of insert fittings and special
crimp rings. Many professional plumbers feel that polybutylene will eventually be
used more frequently than copper for po-
table water systems.

Where to Put the Pipes

The locations for pipes (Illus. 18-1) will vary with the type of fixtures being plumbed. Your plumbing supplier should be able to provide you with a "rough-in book," which will show you exactly where to place your pipes. Exact rough-in measurements usually aren't critical, but they can be, especially with fixtures like pedestal lavatories. While it's impossible to predict exactly where your pipes should go without rough-in specifications, there are some rule-of-thumb figures that will usually work.

Lavatories

Drains for lavatories should come out of the wall about 17″ above the subfloor. The middle of the drain should line up with the middle of the lavatory. If you install a vanity against a side wall (Illus. 18-2) and the middle of the lavatory would be 15″ away from the side wall, the drain should also be about 15″ inches from that wall.

If the drain is roughed-in too low, or too far to the left or right, the problem can be corrected. A tailpiece extension will compensate for a low trap, and fittings can be used to bring the trap arm closer to the fixture trap. If a drain is roughed-in too high, you've got a problem that can't be corrected easily; the only solution to this problem is to rework completely the rough plumbing.

If water pipes for lavatories emerge from a wall, they should be about 21″ above the subfloor. Water pipes that emerge vertically from the floor can be extended as needed. Hot-water pipes should always be installed on the left (as you face the lavatory) side.

Most lavatories have faucets with 4″ centers. This simply means that there's 4″ between the hot and cold water supplies when measured from the middle of one supply tube to the other. If the drain is roughed-in under the middle of the lavatory, each water pipe will be about 2″ from the center of the drain, on each side.

Toilets

Unless you relocate your toilet, you won't have to rough-in a new drain. However, if you install a new closet flange (the part a toilet rests on), the middle of the flange should measure 12½″ out from the wall where the toilet will rest. This measurement is based on measuring from a stud wall. If you measure from a finished wall, the distance should be 12″.

You should be able to measure 15″ from the middle of the closet flange to either side without hitting a wall or another fixture. For proper installation, toilets should have a minimum free width of 30″.

Water supplies for toilets should be installed 6″ above the subfloor, and they should be 6″ to the left of the middle of the drain.

Bathtubs

Drains for bathtubs are typically located 15″ from the stud wall, where the back of the tub will rest. The drain is normally about 4″ from the head wall, where the faucets will go. If you install a new tub drain, cut a hole in the subfloor for the drain before the tub is set in place permanently. The hole should extend 12″ from the head wall, and it should be about 8″ wide, giving you a hole that's 8″ wide and 12″ long. You'll need most of this space to connect a tub waste and overflow to the tub.

Bathtub faucets should be installed about 12″ above the flood-level rim (the arm rest or the spot where the water will first spill over the tub) of the tub. Tub spouts are usually mounted about 4″ above the flood-level rim of the tub.

When you install the faucet for a tub-shower combination, the shower-head outlet should be located about 6' above the subfloor.

Showers

A shower shouldn't be permanently installed until a hole has been cut in the subfloor for the shower drain. Most shower drains are located in the middle of the shower, but there are many types of showers where this isn't the case. Consult a rough-in book, or measure the actual drain location to determine where to rough in the shower drain.

Shower faucets should be installed about 4' above the subfloor.

Kitchen Sinks

The drains for kitchen sinks should emerge from the wall about 15" above the subfloor. As with lavatories, the drain should be near the middle of the sink drain. If you install a double-bowl sink, you only need one drain line. A continuous waste will be used, allowing both bowls to empty into a single trap.

Water supplies for kitchen sinks should emerge from the wall about 18" above the subfloor. The hot water should always be at the left side of the fixture. Most kitchen faucets are made with 8" centers; your water pipes will be spaced 8" apart.

Heating-System Modifications

Heating-system modifications aren't needed in most kitchen and bathroom remodeling jobs. Unless you expand your room, the existing heating system should be adequate, and require no major work. However, there are times, especially with kitchen remodeling, when heat sources have to be relocated within the room. Assuming that there's good access from under the kitchen floor, moving heat usually isn't a big job.

The ducts used in forced-hot-air heating and central air conditioning have very sharp edges when they're disassembled. If you're going to work with heating or air-conditioning ducts, wear gloves.

Ducts are usually held together by metal strips that slide into a channel. These strips can be dislodged with a hammer. Metal fabrication shops will be glad to make lengths of ducts (or offsets) to your specifications. Aside from the risk of cutting yourself on sharp metal, installing duct work isn't difficult.

In some cases, flexible ducts can be used to carry heat or cool air from a main trunk to an outlet register. Flexible ducts are easier to work with than rigid metal ones, and you're not as likely to hurt yourself.

If you add new ducts to an existing system or extend the length of existing ducts, speak with professionals first. Typically, ducts get smaller as they near their final delivery point. If the duct isn't sized correctly, it won't perform optimally. Such duct alterations may influence the effectiveness of your heating and cooling system. New ducts can be cut into existing trunk lines easily, but be sure that your alterations won't strain your system.

Hot-water heat runs through copper tubing similar, if not identical, to the type used for potable water distribution. Don't attempt to work with this type of heat unless you know how to solder. Before you cut into heating pipes, make sure the boiler is turned off and drained down to a point below the pipes you'll be cutting.

There are two types of hot-water heating system: one-pipe systems and two-pipe systems. In a one-pipe system, a supply pipe leaves the boiler and runs to the first heating unit. The water passes through the heating unit and when it comes out, it is conveyed to the next heating unit through supply pipe. Some people refer to this as a "loop" system, because the supply pipe makes a big loop through all of the heating units before returning to the boiler.

Two-pipe systems use supply pipes and return pipes. These systems cost more, due to the extra pipe involved, but they produce better heat than does a one-pipe system. In two-pipe systems, each heating unit receives a supply of hot water from one pipe and another pipe immediately returns the water directly to the boiler.

Adding new heat to an expanded kitchen or bathroom is certainly possible, but you must make sure the boiler is capable of heating the extra space. It's unlikely that any existing boiler won't be able to heat the small amount of space being added in a kitchen or bathroom.

After the new hot-water heating units are installed, bleed the air out of the system. Professionals usually install special elbows, called "vent ells" or "bleed ells," at each heating unit. These fittings are most commonly installed on the heat that has the highest elevation in the home. If your home has more than one story, bleed air from the highest heating units.

To bleed air from the heating system, turn on the boiler, and remove the cap from the bleed fitting. You will probably hear air hissing out of the opening in the fitting. When the air is replaced by a stream of water, you've purged air from the system.

It's usual (with all types of heat) to install heating units on exterior walls, usually under windows. If your house has an old heating system that uses steam or radiators, call in professionals to make the necessary changes in the system. These systems can be troublesome to work with and it isn't unusual for radiators and old steel pipes to fail and leak when disturbed.

Electrical Services

Homeowners sometimes want to (or must) upgrade their electrical service for major remodeling projects. This isn't usually the case with kitchen or bathroom remodeling, but it can be. This isn't a job you should do yourself, unless you're a well-trained electrician, experienced in working with panel boxes. All work with electricity poses some danger, but the risks involved with replacing a service panel are too great for the layman to take.

Installing New Electrical Boxes

Homeowners who feel competent working with electricity can install their own electrical boxes, but if you don't know what you're doing, leave all electrical work to licensed professionals. Poor workmanship with electrical wiring can result in fatal shocks and house fires.

If you'll be installing your own electrical boxes, decide which types to use. The sizes and shapes of electrical boxes vary with their purpose.

Switch Boxes

Switch boxes are usually rectangular, and they're commonly used for wall outlets and wall-mounted lights. Rectangular boxes are generally 3″ by 2″.

Boxes for Ceiling Lights

These boxes, often octagonal, may also be used as junction boxes for joining numerous wires together. Each side of such boxes is typically 4″ long. Round boxes are also used for ceiling lights.

Junction Boxes

Both octagonal and square boxes are used as junction boxes. Square boxes are used more frequently, and they have typical dimensions of about 4″.

Depth Requirements

Depth requirements are determined by the number of wires to be placed in the electrical box. Common depths vary from just over 1″ to about 3½″.

Mounting Electrical Boxes

Some boxes are sold with nails already inserted in them; all you have to do is position the box and drive the nail into a piece of wood. Other boxes have flanges that nails are driven through. Some boxes have flanges that move, allowing for flexibility in placement.

Boxes for ceiling fixtures are often nailed directly to ceiling joists. If the boxes need to be offset, such as in the middle of a joist bay, metal bars can be used to support the boxes. The metal bars are adjustable, and they mount between ceiling joists or studs. Once the bar is in place, the box can be mounted to it.

Rough-In Dimensions

Rough-in dimensions can be determined by local building-code requirements and the fixtures to be served. There are, however, some common rough-in dimensions.

Wall switches are usually mounted about 4′ above the finished floor. Outlets are normally set between 12″ and 18″ above the floor, and are spaced so that there's no more than 12′ between any two outlets.

Where Does the Red Wire Go?

Electrical wires are insulated with colored coatings, which indicate what the wire is used for and where it should be attached.

Black wires and red wires are usually "hot" wires. White wires should be a neutral, but they're sometimes used as hot wires. Don't trust a wire *not* to be hot. Green wires and plain copper wires are usually ground wires.

Match colored wires to the screws in an electrical connection. Black wires should connect to brass screws. Red wires should connect to brass or chrome screws. White wires are normally connected to chrome screws. Green wires and plain copper wires should connect to green screws.

Electrical wires should be crooked and placed under their respective screws in a way that the crook in the wire will tighten with the screw. The end of the crooked wire should face in a clockwise position under the screw.

Wire nuts should be used when wires are twisted together. The colors of wire nuts indicate their size. Wire nuts are plastic on the outside and have wire springs on the inside. When wires are inserted into the wire nut, the nut can be turned clockwise to secure the wires. It's important to use a wire nut of the proper size, and it should be used and tightened so that no bare wiring is visible.

Ground-Fault Interrupters

Ground-fault interrupters (GFIs) are generally required in places where a water source is close to an electrical device. GFIs are safety devices; they turn off the power to an electrical device if moisture is detected. It's possible to install GFI outlets or GFI circuit breakers. Check with your local code-enforcement office to determine the requirements in your area for these devices.

19
Cabinets, Countertops, Fixtures, Trim & Appliances

Cabinets, countertops, fixtures, trim, and appliances must all be installed now. These aspects will determine how the finished job will look. They can also be more difficult to install than they appear to be. When you begin installing these items, be prepared to take your time. Turning a bolt one time too many will break a toilet. Using the wrong screw could cause you to puncture and ruin the surface of a new countertop or cabinet.

As you see all of the cabinets installed in your kitchen, it can be tempting to work into the night to get the countertop installed. The desire to see the top installed before morning could be a mistake. If you're tired, you'll be more likely to make mistakes. The finish work in your project is very important; don't rush it.

Of the items discussed here, cabinets are normally the first to be installed. Cabinet installation requires attention to detail, but it's a job most handy homeowners can do.

Choosing Base Cabinets

Before you choose base cabinets, shop around. You may be amazed at the number of variations available. You'll have to make decisions about sizes, styles, colors, and features.

Cabinets are fundamental to any kitchen. The cabinets will attract more attention than any other feature in the room; they'll also receive a lot of use. Since you'll want your kitchen to be beautiful, functional, and enjoyable, take your time when choosing cabinets.

Standard base cabinets (Illus. 19-1) are generally about 32½″ high. Once a countertop is installed on the base cabinets, the finished height is usually around 36″.

Base cabinets are available in different widths. The base cabinet under the kitchen sink will normally be 5′ wide. Other base cabinets may be as narrow as 12″, or as wide as 36″. There are, of course, other sizes available, and custom cabinets are made to your specifications.

Custom cabinets are generally much more expensive than stock cabinets. With the wide selection of stock cabinets available, there's rarely a need for custom cabinets. Most people will have no trouble finding stock cabinets to suit their needs and desires.

Cabinet materials can consist of solid wood, plywood, and particleboard. Many stock cabinets use a mixture of these materials. Deciding which material you want your cabinets made of is only part of the buying decision. You'll also have to look at the construction features of the cabinets. For example, dovetail joints should last longer than butt joints.

Other considerations for choosing base cabinets include whether the cabinet will have doors, drawers, appliance openings, or special accessories. How well do the drawers glide? Insist on a cabinet with good-quality glides and rollers.

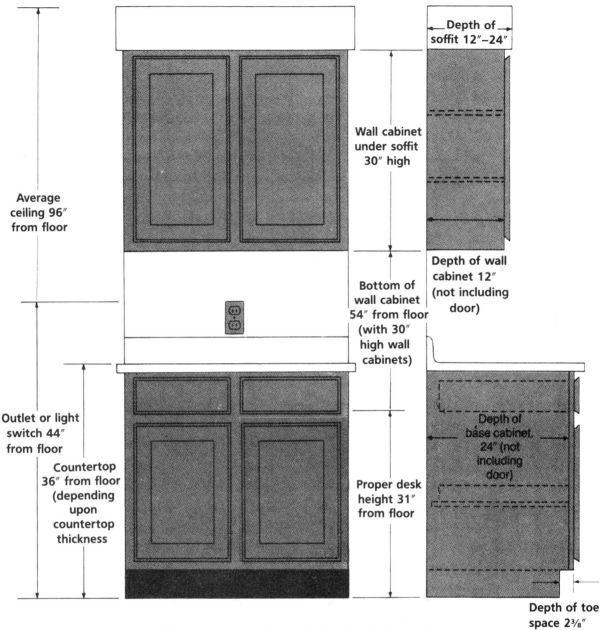

**Illus. 19-1. Typical standard cabinet dimensions.
Drawing courtesy of Merillat Industries**

Choosing Wall Cabinets

Choosing wall cabinets is similar to choosing base cabinets. Consider the sizes and styles that best suit your requirements. Do you want cabinets with glass doors, raised-panel doors, doors with porcelain pulls, or doors with finger grooves? There are many choices to contemplate.

Heights and widths of wall cabinets vary. Most wall cabinets are about 30″ tall. The cabinets used for the space above refrigerators are frequently 15″ tall, and wall cabinets installed over ranges are usually about

18″ tall. Standard widths range from 12″–36″. Different manufacturers offer cabinets in other sizes. When thinking of width, think in 3″ increments, since that's how most wall cabinets are made.

Look for good quality in the shelves and latches of wall cabinets. The supports for shelves should be adjustable and allow random spacing of the shelves. Magnetic latches are usually favored over plastic latches. Inspect hinges, structural supports, and all other structural aspects of wall cabinets before you buy.

Installing Cabinets

Cabinet installation should begin with a design that you've studied and approved. It's much easier to make changes in kitchen design in the design stage than it is while the kitchen is being constructed. You should have a good cabinet layout already drawn. Any good cabinet supplier will provide recommended designs and drawings. When you're ready to install your cabinets, follow the design, but before you jump right into setting and hanging cabinets, double-check your previous work.

Check your floors and walls to make sure that they're plumb and level. Cabinets that aren't installed level may not operate properly, and there may be visual evidence of poor installation. Shims can be used to overcome minor problems with walls and floors.

Installing Wall Cabinets

Install wall cabinets first to reduce the risk of damaging base cabinets. This method will also provide you with freedom of movement.

There are no rules to say how high you must hang your wall cabinets, but most wall cabinets are hung so that the top of the cabinets are about 84″ above the floor. Once

you determine the desired height for your cabinets, mark a level line as a reference point.

Before you put the cabinets in place, find the wall studs. If you gutted your kitchen and installed new drywall, you'll be familiar with the stud locations. You may have even thought ahead and marked their location on your kitchen plan. If you have trouble locating the studs, probe the wall where the cabinets will be hung. The back of the cabinet will conceal any holes you make.

Begin installation by hanging a corner cabinet. Cabinet installation is much easier when at least two people work on the job. Many professionals place props under the cabinets they're hanging to help keep the units in place prior to permanent attachment. The props can be made from leftover lumber from the rough carpentry work.

When the first cabinet is in place and level, drill holes through the back of the cabinet and into the wall studs. The holes should be kept near the top of the cabinet. Most cabinets have mounting strips for the screws to penetrate. Install screws to hold the cabinet in place. Check the unit to make sure that it's level and plumb. If it isn't, use shims to install the cabinet properly.

When the first cabinet is installed, you'll be ready to install adjacent cabinets in the same manner. Adjacent cabinets should be attached to each other. Make sure the cabinets are aligned uniformly. Use small screws to attach the two cabinets to each other. The screws should be installed near the top and bottom of the cabinets' side walls.

If you have help available, you may want to put the cabinets together on the floor and then raise them to the wall as one unit. Take your time when aligning the cabinets. When the cabinets are all attached, simply raise them to the wall and support them with prop sticks. Position the cabinets so that they're level and plumb, and then screw them to the wall studs. If you install a valance, do it before you install the base cabinets.

Installing Base Cabinets

Start with a corner cabinet and build out from the corner, using the remaining cabinets. Base cabinets should be attached to each other just as wall cabinets are. Check frequently to see that the base cabinets are level and plumb. It may be necessary to shim under the cabinets to keep them level.

Not all base cabinets have sides and backs: some are just fronts. This type of unit requires the installation of cleats. Cleats are just strips of wood that support the countertop. The cleats should be attached to wall studs with the top of the cleat at the same height as the tops of the adjacent cabinets.

Installing the Countertop

Once you have the base cabinets installed, it's time for the countertop. Some people wait until the base cabinets are installed before ordering countertops. Working in this manner slows down the job, but it eliminates much of the risk of getting a countertop that isn't the proper size. If you bought your cabinets and countertop from a good supplier, your kitchen layout was probably drawn well in advance, and it's likely that you already have the countertop.

Look down at your base cabinets; you should see some triangular blocks of wood in the corners. These triangles provide a place to attach the counter to the cabinet. Before putting the counter in place, drill holes through these mounting blocks. Keep the holes in a location that will allow you to install screws from inside the cabinet. You may want to drill the holes on an angle, towards the center of the cabinet. This will make installing screws easier.

Position the countertop on the base cabinets, and check its fit. When you're satisfied with the position of the top, install

screws from below. The screws used should be long enough to penetrate the triangular blocks and the bottom of the countertop, but be certain that they're not long enough to emerge through to the surface of the counter and ruin it.

Kitchen counters must have a hole cut in them for the kitchen sink. The supplier of the top will often cut these holes if you provide him with the size of the sink. If you must cut your own sink hole, use the template that came with your new sink. If you don't have a template to work with, turn the sink upside down and put it in place on the counter.

With a pencil, lightly trace around the sink rim. Remove the sink and draw a new outline inside the original tracing. The hole must be smaller than the lines you traced around the sink. There must be enough counter left after the hole is cut to support the rim of the sink.

When you're ready to cut out the sink hole, drill a hole in the countertop, within the perimeter of the sink hole. Use a jig saw to cut out the sink hole. Put the blade in the hole you drilled and slowly cut the hole. Remember, the hole you make must be smaller than the outline of the sink. After the hole is cut, set the sink in it and check the fit; you may have to enlarge the hole a little at a time to get a perfect fit.

Installing Interior Trim

Installing interior trim isn't difficult, but it does require precise measurements and patience. A miter box and a backsaw will be needed for cutting the angles required for interior trim. Once you get used to cutting angles, installing trim won't be much of a chore.

Baseboard trim (Illus. 19-2) should be nailed to wall studs, using small finish nails. When baseboard trim meets a door casing or a cabinet, it simply butts against the cas-

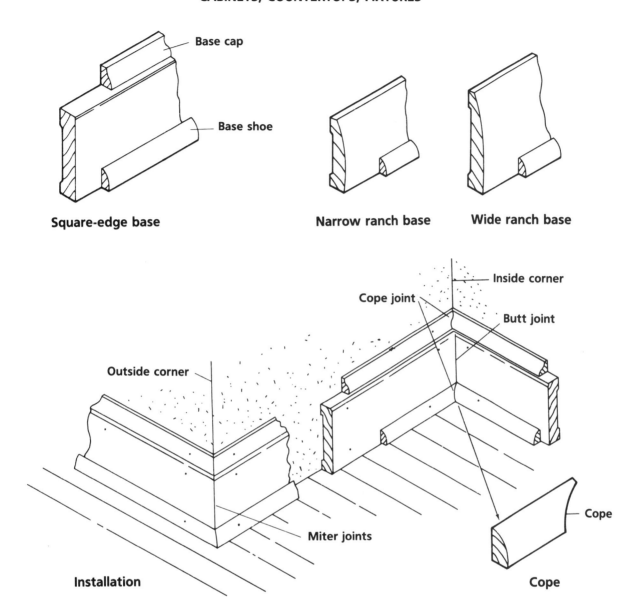

Illus. 19-2. Base moldings. Drawing courtesy of USDA Forest Service

ing or cabinet. Shoe molding is generally installed with baseboard trim when vinyl flooring is used. Shoe molding is small trim that installs in front of baseboard trim. It's often used to cover the joints where vinyl flooring meets a baseboard. If flooring was installed before the baseboard trim, shoe molding is unnecessary.

Windows, doors, and open entryways are often trimmed with casing (Illustrations 19-

3, 19-4, 19-5). The only trick to installing this trim is to cut the proper angles, and a miter box will make that part of the job nearly foolproof.

The nails installed in trim should be countersunk. A nail punch can be used to drive the nail heads deep into the trim. Putty should then be placed in the nail holes before the final paint or stain work is done. If the trim is to be stained, make sure it's made

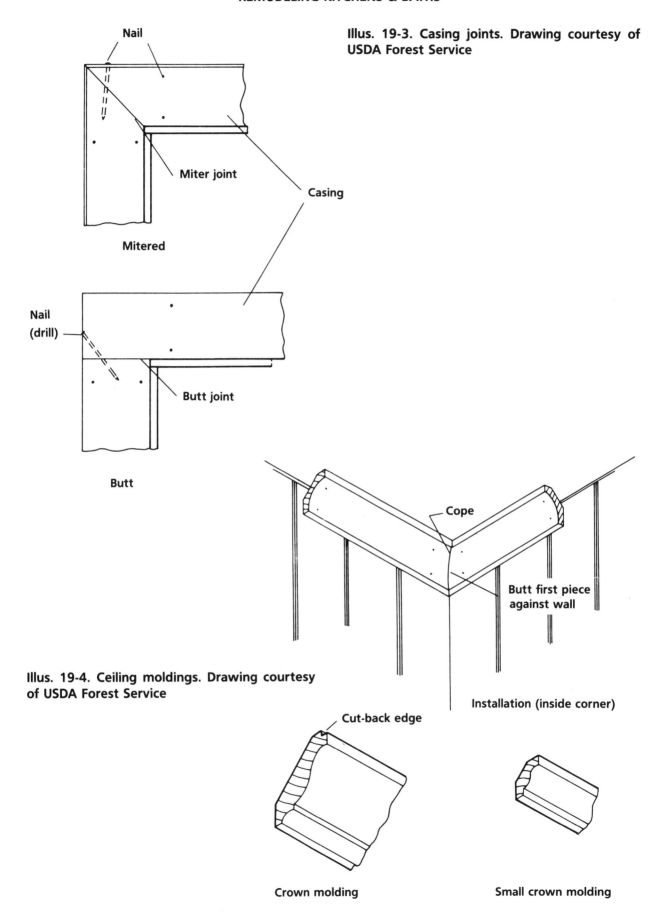

Nail

Nail

Miter joint

Casing

Mitered

Nail
(drill)

Butt joint

Butt

Cope

Butt first piece
against wall

Installation (inside corner)

Cut-back edge

Crown molding

Small crown molding

Illus. 19-3. Casing joints. Drawing courtesy of USDA Forest Service

Illus. 19-4. Ceiling moldings. Drawing courtesy of USDA Forest Service

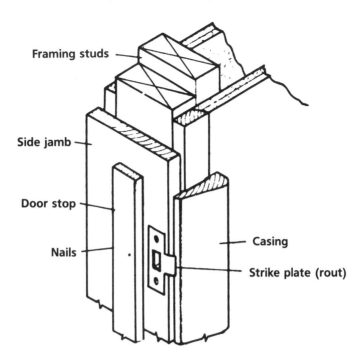

**Illus. 19-5. Door-trim and strike-plate detail.
Drawing courtesy of USDA Forest Service**

of clear wood, and that the putty won't show through the stain.

Setting Plumbing Fixtures

When you're ready to set plumbing fixtures, the end of your job is in sight. Some plumbing fixtures, such as toilets, must be handled with care, but installing most plumbing fixtures isn't very difficult.

Toilets

Toilets rest on and are bolted to closet flanges. Unless you've relocated the drain for your toilet, you should be able to use the existing closet flange. If you must install a new closet flange, install it so that the slots in the flange will allow the closet bolts to sit on either side of the middle of the drain. The top of the flange should be flush with the finish flooring. If it is only slightly above the flooring you shouldn't have any prob-

lems, but if it's too high above the floor, the toilet won't mount properly.

Place closet bolts in the grooves of the flange and line them up with the middle of the drain. Now install a wax ring over the drain opening in the flange, and set the toilet bowl on the wax and press down firmly. The closet bolts should come up through the mounting holes in the base of the toilet.

Measure the distance from the back wall to the holes in the toilet where the seat will be installed. The two holes should be at an equal distance from the back wall. If they aren't, adjust the bowl until they are.

Install the flat plastic caps (that came with the toilet) over the closet bolts. If metal washers were packed with the closet bolts, install them next. Install the closet-bolt nuts, and tighten them *carefully*: Too much stress will break the bowl. Snap the plastic cover caps (that came with the toilet) over the bolts and onto the flat plastic disks you installed over the closet bolts. If the bolts

173

are too long to allow the caps to fit, cut off the bolts, using a hacksaw.

Uncrate the toilet tank, and install the large sponge washer over the threaded piece that extends from the bottom of the tank. Then install the tank-to-bowl bolts. To do this, slide the heavy black washers over the bolts until they reach the heads of the bolts. Push the bolts through the toilet tank.

Pick up the tank and set it in place on the bowl. The sponge gasket and bolts should line up with the holes in the bowl. With the tank in place, slide metal washers over the tank-to-bowl bolts from beneath the bowl. Follow the washers with nuts, and tighten them carefully, since too much stress will crack the tank. Alternate between bolts as you tighten them. This allows the pressure to be applied evenly, reducing the chance of breakage. Tighten the bolts until the tank won't twist and turn on the bowl. Now you'll be ready to connect the water supply.

Turn off the water to the toilet's supply pipe. Cut off the supply pipe about ¾″ above the floor or past the wall, depending upon where the pipe originates. Slide an escutcheon over the pipe, and install a cut-off valve. Compression valves require the least amount of skill and effort to install.

Install a closet supply between the cut-off valve and the ballcock (the threads protruding past the bottom of the tank, in the left front corner). Polybutylene closet supplies are the easiest type to install, but only nylon compression ferrules should be used with polybutylene supplies. Remove the ballcock nut from the threads at the bottom of the toilet tank. Hold a closet supply in place, and, after measuring it, cut it to a suitable length.

Slide the ballcock nut onto the supply tube, with the threads facing the toilet tank. Slide the small nut from the cut-off valve onto the supply tube and follow it with the compression ferrule. Hold the supply up to the ballcock and tighten the ballcock nut. Insert the other end of the supply into the cut-off valve. Slide the ferrule and compression nut down to the threads on the cut-off, and tighten the nut. Then tighten the large ballcock nut.

Toilet seats generally have built-in bolts that fit through holes in the bowl. Put the seat in place and tighten the nuts that hold it in place.

This completes the toilet installation. After turning the water on, flush the toilet several times and check all connections to make sure that none leak.

Installing the Lavatory

How you install your lavatory will depend on the type of lavatory you have. Drop-in lavatories require a hole to be cut in the counter in which they'll be mounted. The bowls are set in the hole and are held in place by their weight and plumbing connections. A bead of caulking should be placed around the hole, on the surface of the counter, before you set the lavatory in place.

Rimmed lavatories also require a hole to be cut in the countertop, but they aren't as easy to install as drop-in lavatories. Rimmed lavatories have a metal rim that's placed in the hole of the countertop. The lavatory bowl is then held up to the ring, from below, and secured with special clips.

Wall-hung lavatories hang on wall brackets. Wood backing must be installed during the rough-in phase so that there will be a firm surface to which to bolt the wall bracket. Once the wall bracket is mounted, most wall-hung lavatories simply rest on the bracket. A few types have additional mounting holes where lag bolts can be used to provide additional security, so that the bowl won't be knocked off the wall bracket. Most wall-hung lavatories are made to accept legs, but legs are optional.

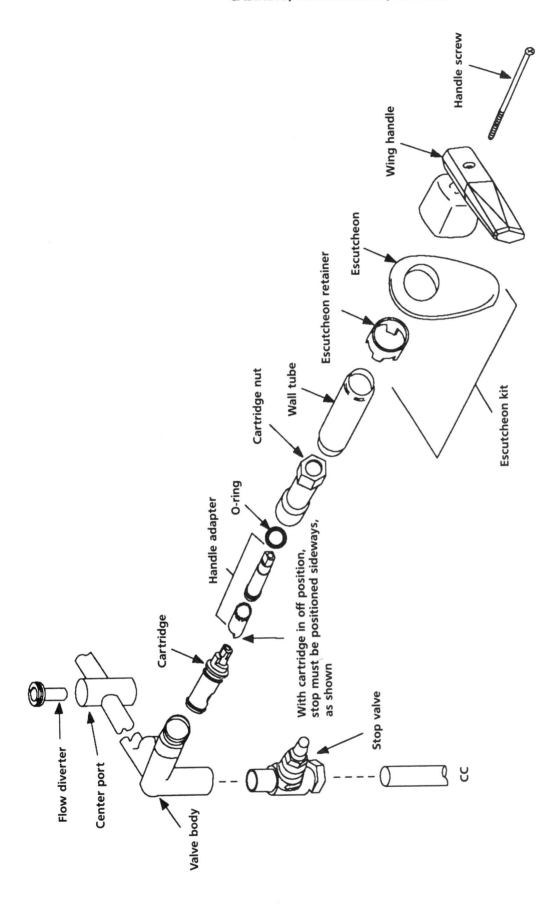

Illus. 19-6. Exploded view of a shower valve. Drawing courtesy of Moen, Inc.

Vanity tops with the lavatory bowl built into the top are the easiest to install. These tops simply rest on a vanity cabinet. The tops are usually heavy enough to sit in place without needing any special attachments.

Lavatory Faucets & Drains

Most standard lavatory faucets and drains are assembled alike. This job will be easy if you mount the faucet and drain assembly before you install the lavatory. A basin wrench may be necessary when working with faucets; you can buy such a wrench inexpensively at any tool store.

Many faucets come with gaskets that fit between the base of the faucet and the lavatory. If your faucet doesn't have one of these gaskets, make a gasket from plumber's putty. Roll the putty into a long, round line and place it around the perimeter of the faucet base.

Place the faucet on the lavatory with the threaded fittings going through the holes. Slide the ridged washers over the threaded fittings of the faucet, and then screw on the mounting nuts. Tighten these nuts until the faucet is firmly seated.

Lavatory supply tubes mount on the ends of the threaded fittings protruding below the lavatory. Slide supply nuts up the supply tubes and screw them onto the threaded fittings. The beveled heads of the lavatory supplies prevent leaks.

Now you're ready to connect the drain. First assemble and install the pop-up drain assembly. Detailed instructions for proper installation should be packed with your faucet. Read and follow the manufacturer's instructions.

A pop-up assembly mounts in the hole in the bottom of a lavatory. Unscrew the round trim piece from the shaft of the pop-up. (This is the piece you see when you look into a lavatory.) Roll up some plumber's putty and place a ring of it around the bottom of the trim piece. Slide down the fat, tapered, black washer that's on the threaded portion of the assembly onto the threaded shaft. You may have to loosen the big nut that's on the threads to get the metal washer and rubber washer to move down onto the assembly.

Apply pipe dope or a sealant tape to the threads of the pop-up assembly. With your hand under the lavatory bowl, push the threaded assembly up through the drainage hole. Screw the small trim piece (the one with the putty on it) onto the threads. Push the tapered gasket up to the bottom of the lavatory. Tighten the mounting nut until it pushes the metal washer up to the rubber washer and compresses the rubber washer. You should see putty being squeezed out from under the trim ring as you tighten the nut.

When the mounting nut is tight, the metal pop-up rod that extends from the assembly should be pointing to the rear of the lavatory bowl. Take the thin metal rod (used to open and close the drain) and push it through the small hole in the middle of the faucet.

You should see a thin metal clip on the end of the rod that extends from the pop-up assembly. Remove the first edge of this clip from the round rod. Take the perforated metal strip that was packed with the pop-up and slide it over the pop-up rod. You can use any of the holes for starters. Now, slide the edge of the thin metal clip back onto the pop-up rod to hold the perforated strip in place.

At the other end of the perforated strip there will be a hole and a setscrew. Loosen the setscrew and slide the pop-up rod (used to open and close the drain) through the hole. Hold the rod so that about 1½" of it protrudes above the top of the faucet. Tighten the setscrew. Pull up on the pop-up rod to see if it operates the pop-up plug. The pop-up plug is the stopper in the sink drain. You can test this best after all connections are made to the water and drainage systems.

There should be a 1¼″ chrome tailpiece (round tubular piece) packed with the pop-up assembly. The tailpiece will have fine threads on one end and no threads on the other. Coat the threads with pipe dope or sealant tape. Screw the tailpiece into the bottom of the pop-up assembly.

Now you're ready to install the trap. First, slide an escutcheon over the trap arm (the pipe coming out of the wall). Lavatory traps are normally 1¼″; however, you can use a 1½″ trap with a reducing nut on the end that connects to the tailpiece. Assuming you used plastic pipe for your rough-in, you may either glue the trap directly to the trap arm (if you use a schedule-forty trap), or you may use a trap adapter. A trap adapter will be needed if the trap is metal and the trap arm is plastic. Trap adapters glue onto pipe, just like any other fitting. One end of the adapter is equipped with threads, to accept a slip-nut.

Start by placing the trap on the tailpiece. To do this, remove the slip-nut from the vertical section of the trap. Slide the slip-nut onto the tailpiece and follow it with the washer that was under it; the washer may be nylon or rubber. Put the trap on the tailpiece, and check the alignment with the trap arm. It may be necessary to use a fitting to offset the trap arm in the direction of the trap.

If the trap is below the trap arm, you'll have to shorten the tailpiece. The tailpiece is best cut using a pair of roller-cutters, but it can be cut with a hacksaw. You may have to remove the tailpiece to cut it. If the trap is too high, you can use a tailpiece extension to lower it. A tailpiece extension is a tubular section that fits between the trap and the tailpiece. The extension may be plastic or metal, and it's held in place with slip-nuts and washers.

Once the trap is at the proper height, de-termine if the trap arm needs to be cut or extended. Extending the trap arm can be done with a regular coupling and pipe section. If you use a schedule-forty plastic trap, it is glued onto the trap arm. If you use a metal trap, the long section of the trap will slip into a trap adapter. You may have to shorten the length of the trap's horizontal section. When using a trap adapter, slide the slip-nut and washer on the trap section; then insert the trap section into the adapter and secure it by tightening the slip-nut. Once the trap-to-trap-arm connection is complete, tighten the slip-nut at the tailpiece.

With the water turned off to the supply pipes, install the cut-offs for the lavatory. Remove the aerator (the piece screwed onto the faucet spout) from the faucet. If you don't remove the aerator before you run water through the faucet for the first time, the faucet might become blocked with debris, causing an erratic water stream. Other than to test for leaks, your work with the lavatory is done.

Installing Tub & Shower Trim

Installing tub and shower trim is easy, but connecting a tub waste and overflow is difficult, if you don't have any help.

Shower Trim

To install shower trim, start with the shower head. Be sure the main water supply is turned off, and unscrew the stub-out from the shower-head ell. Slide the escutcheon that came with the shower assembly over the shower arm. Apply pipe dope or sealant tape to the threads on each end of the shower arm. Screw the shower head onto the short section of the arm, where the bend is. Screw the long section of the arm into the threaded ell in the wall.

Use an adjustable wrench, on the flats around the shower head, to tighten all connections. If you must use pliers on the arm, keep them close to the wall, so that the escutcheon will hide any scratch marks.

Now you're ready to trim the shower valve (Illus. 19-6). How this is done depends upon the type of faucet you roughed in. Follow manufacturer's suggestions. If you installed a single-handle unit, you'll usually install a large escutcheon first. These escutcheons have a foam gasket, eliminating the need for plumber's putty. The handle is installed and the cover cap is snapped into place over the handle screw.

If you use a two-handle faucet, you'll generally screw chrome collars over the faucet stems. These may be followed by escutcheons, or the escutcheons may be integral parts of the sleeves. Putty should be placed where the escutcheons come into contact with the tub wall, and then the handles installed.

Tub Faucets

Tub faucets are trimmed in the same way as are shower faucets. However, you have to install a tub spout. Some tub spouts slide over a piece of copper tubing and are held in place with a setscrew. Many tub spouts have female-threaded connections either at the inlet or the outlet of the spout. If you have a threaded connection, you must solder a male adapter onto the stub-out from your tub valve, or use a threaded ell and galvanized nipple. The easiest type of spout to install is one that slides over the copper and attaches with a setscrew. Place plumber's putty on the tub spout where the spout comes into contact with the tub wall.

Tub Wastes

Tub wastes are difficult to install when you work alone. The tub waste and overflow can take several forms. It may be made of metal or plastic. It can use a trip lever, a push button, a twist-and-turn stopper, or an old-fashioned rubber stopper. The tub waste may be joined with slip-nuts or glued joints. Follow the directions that come with the tub waste.

First, mount the drain. Unscrew the chrome drain from the tub shoe. You'll see a thick black washer. Install a ring of putty around the chrome drain, and apply pipe dope to the threads. Hold the tub shoe under the tub so that it lines up with the drain hole. Screw the chrome drain into the female threads of the shoe. The black washer should be on the bottom of the tub, between the tub and the shoe. Once the chrome drain is tight, leave it alone for the time being.

The tub shoe has a tubular drainage pipe extending from it. Make this drain point toward the head of the tub, where the faucets are. Take the tee that came with the tub waste and put it on the drainage tube from the shoe. The long drainage tube that will accept the tub's overflow should be placed in the top of the tee. The face of the overflow tube should line up with the overflow hole in the tub. Cut the tubing on the overflow or shoe as needed for a proper fit. The cuts are best made with roller-cutters, but they can be made using a hacksaw.

You should have a sponge gasket in your assortment of parts. This gasket will be placed on the face of the overflow tubing, between the back of the tub and the overflow head. From inside the bathtub, install the faceplate for the overflow. For trip-lever styles, fish the trip mechanism down the overflow tubing. For other types of tub wastes, you'll only have a cover plate to screw on. Tighten the screws until the sponge gasket is compressed.

Now tighten the drain. This can be done by crossing two large screwdrivers and using them between the crossbars of the drain. Turn the drain clockwise until the putty spreads out from under the drain. The last step is to connect the tub waste to the trap. This can be done with trap adapters or glue joints, depending upon the type of tub waste you use.

Apply joint compound to the threads of the tailpiece. If you're using a metal waste, screw the tailpiece into place. Now the procedure will be exactly like that used to hook up a lavatory drain.

Installing the Kitchen Sink

Installing the kitchen sink is similar to installing the lavatory, but there are differences. Some kitchen sinks are drop-ins. Like lavatories, drop-in sinks don't require clips, only caulking. Most sinks, however, are held in place with clips. These clips slide into a channel that runs around the rim of the sink. As the clips are tightened, usually with a screwdriver, the clips bite into the bottom of the countertop, pulling the sink firmly into contact with the top of the counter. There are different types of sink clamps, so check your materials and manufacturer's instructions for proper installation.

Instead of pop-up assemblies, kitchen sinks use basket strainers for drains. Putty is applied around the rim of the drain and the drain is pushed through the hole in the sink. From below, a gasket is slid over the threaded portion of the drain and a large nut is applied and tightened. These nuts can be difficult to tighten without help. It is best to have someone cross screwdrivers in the crossbars of the basket strainer as the nut is being tightened. Otherwise, the entire drain assembly tends to turn, without becoming tight.

A good solution for the person working alone is a type of drain that uses a flange to secure the basket strainer. This flange slides over the threads and is held against the bottom of the sink by three pressure points.

The pressure points are threaded rods, extending from another flange that's screwed onto the drain threads. As the threaded rods are tightened, they apply pressure and seal the drain.

Kitchen tailpieces don't screw into the basket strainers. Instead, they're flanged to accept tailpiece washers. The nylon washer sits atop the tailpiece, and the tailpiece is held in place with a slip-nut.

Since many kitchen sinks have two bowls, continuous wastes are often used to drain the two bowls to a common trap. There are end-outlet wastes and center-outlet wastes. The continuous waste attaches to the sink's tailpieces with slip-nuts and washers. Then the waste tubes run either to a tee, for an end-outlet waste, or to a double tee, for a center-outlet waste. The bottom of these tees accepts a tailpiece and allows the trap to be attached.

Appliances

Ranges and refrigerators are easy to install, if you follow the manufacturer's recommendations. However, dishwashers and garbage disposers are combined with both the plumbing and the electrical systems, and it may help to have a little extra information about these appliances.

Garbage Disposers

Garbage disposers are mounted to kitchen sinks, and they replace basket strainers. Putty is applied to the ring of the disposer's trim piece before the trim is pushed through the drain hole. A pressure-type flange is put over the collar of the drain, followed by a snap ring. The snap ring holds the pressure flange in place. Threaded rods are tightened with a screwdriver to seal the drain. The disposer is held in place, and a rotating collar is turned to lock the disposer firmly to the sink flange.

Disposers have small ells that come with them. Two screws are loosened on the side of the disposer. The ell fits through a metal housing and a rubber washer is placed on the beveled end of the ell (the short end). The metal housing is put back in place, and the screws are tightened. This compresses the gasket between the face of the ell and the side of the disposer. Then a continuous waste or trap is connected to the bottom of the disposer ell.

Dishwashers

Dishwashers are usually installed under countertops, between cabinets. There are metal tabs at the top of dishwashers that allow screws to be installed to hold the appliance in place. A rubber drain hose connects to a ridged nylon drain on the appliance. The hose is held in place by a snap ring or clamp. This hose should run into the sink base and rise to the top of the enclosure. It should connect (with clamps) to an air gap.

An air gap is a device that rests on the counter and has a chrome cover. To install it, remove the chrome cover and mounting nut. The unit is pushed up through a hole from beneath the counter. Then a gasket and mounting nut are installed and tightened. Afterwards, the chrome cover is replaced. Below the counter, the air gap splits off into a wye.

The small hose from the dishwasher connects to one side of the wye and is held in place with a clamp. A larger hose is run from the other section of the wye to a wye-tail-piece connection or a connection point on a disposer. If you are connecting to a disposer, you must knock out the factory-installed plug before connecting the hose. This can be done with a sturdy screwdriver and a hammer. You should knock out this plug before installing the disposer; otherwise, retrieving the knocked-out plug will be difficult.

To connect the water supply to the dishwasher, use a dishwasher stop or cut a tee into the hot-water supply to the sink. A dishwasher stop has provisions for a supply tube to the sink and the tubing running to the dishwasher. The copper tubing for the dishwasher should be equipped with a cut-off valve. If you use a dishwasher stop, you have a built-in cut-off. If you cut in a tee, install a cut-off valve between the tee and the dishwasher.

The tubing will run to a point under the dishwasher. A dishwasher ell is used to make the connection between the tubing and the dishwasher. The dishwasher ell screws into the dishwasher. Use pipe dope or tape on the threads. The tubing connects to the ell with a compression nut and ferrule.

Installing Electrical Fixtures & Devices

Installing electrical fixtures and devices is simple, but due to the risk of electrocution, caution must be observed. Never trust a wire until it's been tested with a meter.

Installing Wiring Devices

When installing wiring devices, there's a color-code system that should be followed. Green wires or bare copper wires should be used as ground wires and attached to green screws. Red wires should be considered hot wires and will normally attach to brass or chrome screws. Black wires are also considered hot and generally attach to brass screws. In many cases white wires serve as neutral wires and connect to chrome screws; but don't count on white wires not being hot. For details, glance back to page 166.

Wall Plates & Switch Covers

Wall plates and switch covers simply mount

over outlet boxes and switch boxes. They're held in place with screws.

Installing Light Fixtures

Installing light fixtures is usually a matter of matching up feed wires with fixture wires and then mounting the fixture. Most fixtures have threaded studs that hold them to their electrical box. Follow the manufacturer's recommendations that come with your light fixtures.

20
As the Dust Settles

By now, you'll either be tired of remodeling, or elated with your success. Now you have to peel off the stickers from fixtures, remove the big black letters from vinyl flooring, and pull packing material out of the new refrigerator. This is a glorious time for remodelers. This is also a time when many avoidable accidents happen to put a damper on the jubilation of a job well done.

All too often remodelers let their guard down near the end of a job. A razor blade is used by an eager remodeler to remove a sticker from a fiberglass bathtub, and the tub is so scratched that fiberglass repair is required. The remodeler wrestles with a new refrigerator, trying to get it into place and the new kitchen floor is torn. Many disasters lurk at the end of a job.

To avoid last-minute problems with your remodeling project, you'll have to stay alert and attentive to what you're doing.

Vinyl Floors

Vinyl floors can be cut or torn when you install appliances. To avoid this disaster, cover the new flooring with cardboard while you install the appliances.

The bold black letters on vinyl flooring can be removed using standard household cleaners. Mix warm water with a floor cleaner, and then use a sponge mop to make the marks disappear.

If a new vinyl floor develops bubbles in its surface, use a straight pin to pop the bubble and release trapped air.

Countertops

Countertops can be cleaned with standard household cleaners, but avoid heavy abrasives.

Walls

Walls are frequently abused during the final phases of remodeling. Touching up the paint won't take long, but the touch-up should be feathered out to conceal its presence. If you just dab a little paint on a marred surface, the repair will be obvious. Apply a thin coat of paint to an area large enough so that the new paint blends in well.

Nicks and small holes in the walls can be filled with drywall compound, and then sanded and painted.

Ceilings

Ceilings can suffer marks and holes from baseboard trim being banged into them during trim installation. Ceilings can be repaired using the same techniques as described above for walls.

Light Fixtures

Light fixtures aren't sold with light bulbs. Remember to buy light bulbs. Check the fixtures for wattage ratings, and don't exceed the recommended wattage when you install light bulbs.

Windows

New windows are often covered with stickers, which can be removed quickly, using a straight-edged razor blade. Use a holder for the razor blade to avoid cutting your fingers.

Plumbing Fixtures

Plumbing fixtures frequently have stickers attached to them. Hot water is the best way to remove these stickers. A razor blade can be used, but don't scratch the fixture's finish.

Installing Accessories

You'll usually install accessories at the end of the job. In a bathroom remodeling, the accessories might be towel rings, towel racks, shower curtains, doors, toothbrush holders, soap holders, toilet-paper holders, and so forth. Kitchen accessories might be under-cabinet can openers, under-cabinet coffee makers, curtain rods, and so on.

These accessories can cause a lot of grief. If you make a hole in a new wall at the wrong location, it will have to be patched and painted. Don't install accessories on impulse. Plan for them, just as you planned for the major parts of your job. If you are unable to attach the accessories to wall studs, use screws and expanding anchors to secure them to your drywall. Take the time to ensure that appropriate accessories, like towel racks, are level. Negligence at this stage could be costly.

Cleaning

When you clean up, be aware of your new walls, fixtures, windows, and cabinets. A mop handle can do a lot of damage if it jabs a window or wall. Even if the handle doesn't knock a hole in your new wall, it can leave a long streak on the finished surface.

Don't use abrasive cleaners on your plumbing fixtures, floors, or countertops. The heavy grit in these cleaners isn't needed with new fixtures, and it can damage them.

Remove all debris from your job before you do your touch-up work. Cardboard boxes and leftover lumber can mar newly painted walls.

Don't sweep or clean your room immediately after doing paint touch-up work. The fresh paint will act like a dust magnet.

Final Inspection

Do a final inspection on your work both during the day and at night. Flaws that go unnoticed in one type of light will show up in another. Check all plumbing connections closely for leaks. Test all electrical outlets and fixtures. Go back to your production schedule and note the work you've done, and then check all of the work to make sure it's satisfactory. Inspect your work closely, and tend to any corrections immediately. If you put off fixing something, it may remain uncorrected for months.

When you're satisfied that all of the job is complete and satisfactory, invite the local code-enforcement office to make a final inspection. Final inspections often involve different inspectors. You may see a plumbing inspector, an electrical inspector, a heating inspector, and a building inspector. A fire inspector may even visit. Get these inspections done and retain the final approvals for your files.

Acknowledgments

I thank my mother and my father, Maralou and Woody, for their many years of support, help, and advice.

I also thank the following companies for loaning the illustrations that appear in this book:

American Olean Tile Company
Lansdale, PA 19446-0271

Armstrong World Industries, Inc.
Lancaster, PA 17604-3001

Azrock Industries, Inc.
San Antonio, TX 78269

Benjamin Moore & Co.
Montvale, NJ 07645

Clairson International
Ocala, FL 32674

Decora'
Jasper, IN 47547-0420

Du Pont
Wilmington, DE 19898

Georgia-Pacific Corporation
Atlanta, GA 30348-5606

Jenn-Air Company
Indianapolis, IN 46226-0901

Lis King Public Relations
Mahwah, NJ 07430

Mannington Resilient Floors
Salem, NJ 08079-0030

Marvin Windows and Doors
Warroad, MN 56763

Merillat Industries
(Drucilla Handy Co. Marketing Public Relations)
Chicago, IL 60601-3903

Moen, Inc.
Elyria, OH 44036-2111

NuTone, Incorporated
Cincinnati, OH 45227-1599

Owens-Corning
Toledo, OH 43659

Pittsburgh Corning Corp.
(Westhead Marketing Communications)
Pittsburgh, PA 15222-1442

Plain 'n Fancy Custom Cabinetry
Schaefferstown, PA 17088

Quaker Maid, a division of WCI, Inc.
Leesport, PA 19533-9984

The Tileworks
Des Moines, IA 50312

United States Dept. of Agriculture Forest Service
Washington, DC 20250

United States Gypsum Company
Chicago, IL 60680-4124

Velux-America Inc.
Greenwood, SC 29648

Ralph Wilson Plastics Co.
Temple, TX 76503-6110

Wilsonart
Temple, TX 76503-6110

Wood-Mode, Inc.
Kreamer, PA 17833

Metric Equivalents

INCHES TO MILLIMETRES AND CENTIMETRES

MM—millimetres   *CM—centimetres*

Inches	MM	CM	Inches	CM	Inches	CM
⅛	3	0.3	9	22.9	30	76.2
¼	6	0.6	10	25.4	31	78.7
⅜	10	1.0	11	27.9	32	81.3
½	13	1.3	12	30.5	33	83.8
⅝	16	1.6	13	33.0	34	86.4
¾	19	1.9	14	35.6	35	88.9
⅞	22	2.2	15	38.1	36	91.4
1	25	2.5	16	40.6	37	94.0
1¼	32	3.2	17	43.2	38	96.5
1½	38	3.8	18	45.7	39	99.1
1¾	44	4.4	19	48.3	40	101.6
2	51	5.1	20	50.8	41	104.1
2½	64	6.4	21	53.3	42	106.7
3	76	7.6	22	55.9	43	109.2
3½	89	8.9	23	58.4	44	111.8
4	102	10.2	24	61.0	45	114.3
4½	114	11.4	25	63.5	46	116.8
5	127	12.7	26	66.0	47	119.4
6	152	15.2	27	68.6	48	121.9
7	178	17.8	28	71.1	49	124.5
8	203	20.3	29	73.7	50	127.0

Index

Bold figures indicate pages where illustrations can be found.

About the Author

R. Dodge Woodson, a seasoned veteran of kitchen and bathroom remodeling, is licensed as a master plumber and as a general contractor. In his twenty-one years in the business, Dodge has seen and done just about everything involved in remodeling kitchens and baths.

Woodson's knowledge comes from experience. He has driven nails, soldered pipes, laid tile, set cabinets, and worked with all the other components of remodeling, from basic to exotic.

The author, his wife, Kimberley, and their daughter, Afton, live in rural Maine and enjoy a quiet, New England life-style.